SPRING LAKE HEIGHTS

SPRING LAKE HEIGHTS

A BRIEF HISTORY

LISSA WICKHAM-MCGRATH

THE History PRESS

Published by The History Press
Charleston, SC 29403
www.historypress.net

Front cover: Postcard image courtesy of John Miller.
Back cover: Lily Ann Tea Room image courtesy of Jean Worthington.
Graduation image courtesy of the Veltre family.

First published 2012

Manufactured in the United States

ISBN 978.1.60949.045.4

Library of Congress CIP data applied for.

CONTENTS

ACKNOWLEDGEMENTS

I would like to express my deepest appreciation to the following individuals, whose patience and kind cooperation helped to make this book possible: Eric Bennett, Lori Carloni, Evelyn Condello, Dawn and Howard Eckman, Ann Gardella, David Gee, Jane Hall, Barbara Kolarsick Harrigan, Leona Haviland, Betty Shipper Hosner, the Reverend Dr. Marion Jackson, Marilyn Krampert, John Miller, Ralph and Margie Newman, Michael Pazienza, Doug Polictro, Gary Rice, the Shipper family, Keith Smith, Frank and Janice Veltre, Carole and Jay Wickham and Jean Worthington.

My gratitude extends to the staffs of the Asbury Park Library and the Monmouth County Historical Association, who offered gracious assistance with my research.

Thank you to Albert Weierman and also to the staff at the Frank E. Adams Municipal Building.

And last but not least, I want to thank my husband, Frederic McGrath, for his love, support and patience.

INTRODUCTION

From its tree-lined streets and appealing neighborhoods to its recreational parks and golf course views, Spring Lake Heights is considered by many to be one of the Jersey Shore's most friendly and attractive communities.

Given its many attributes, it came as little surprise when, in April 2006, a leading New Jersey magazine first included the town on its list of the top one hundred places to live in the state. For the borough's little more than five thousand residents, the magazine's recognition merely confirmed what they had already come to know.

Spring Lake Heights may have had a very humble beginning, but the borough has fully blossomed since its incorporation in 1927.

In addition to the town's amenities, history is found here, too, especially along State Highway 71, where horse-drawn carriages were once a common sight. Today, modest professional buildings stand close to century-old homes on what was earlier known as the Squan Turnpike and then, later, State Highway 4N.

Here, on a busy corner, an Irish pub has been converted from a former stagecoach stop and tavern, while in a nearby neighborhood a historic church building has been refurbished and now is used as a Masonic lodge. The borough is a blend of the old and new, with certain parts of its past having been reinvented to fit the present and future.

Spring Lake Heights was created from two small but unique villages: Villa Park and Lake Como. Whereas Villa Park was founded as a summer resort, Lake Como was known primarily as a farming community, whose original settlers had ties to the Revolutionary War.

This book invites readers to explore the historical aspects of these former villages and then to travel through the ensuing decades as this small town took shape.

As the borough's story has unfolded throughout the years, one point has remained consistent and clear: its residents have nurtured a caring community whose proud heritage can be passed on to the future.

I

THE LENNI-LENAPE IN NEW JERSEY

The first known inhabitants of New Jersey—and, in particular, Monmouth County—were the Lenni-Lenape Indians, a Delaware Indian tribe of the Algonquin race.

The earliest Lenni-Lenape migrated from lands far west of the Mississippi River. As the Lenape traveled east in search of a new homeland, they encountered another large Native American tribe, the Mengwe, later known as the Iroquois. Upon meeting, the two tribes appear to have established a friendship and continued their long journey together.

After they successfully battled against the savage Allegheny Indians, the two tribes settled in eastern Pennsylvania, where they peacefully coexisted for many years. Ultimately, the tribes parted company as the Iroquois made their way north to the Great Lakes region and the Lenape slowly continued their trek eastward.

As they crossed over the Delaware River and into New Jersey, the Lenape found a relatively mild climate and a land that was lush in vegetation. While the majority of the tribe relocated north of Red Bank, there were many smaller groups, consisting of twenty-five to thirty members each, who migrated into lower Monmouth County and points south of the Manasquan River. Typically, these settlements were established near streams, rivers or other bodies of water where there was an easy accessibility to fishing, bathing and travel. The Lenape navigated these waterways in dugout canoes. Most settlements were also located near woods for hunting purposes.

The Indians were migratory and spent spring through autumn in areas close to the shore. In all probability, the Lenape passed through Spring Lake Heights while en route to the beach to harvest shellfish. The woods and wetlands surrounding Wreck Pond undoubtedly offered an ample supply of animals and waterfowl for their needs.

In later years, evidence of Indian camps would be uncovered in Brielle and Manasquan and at various spots in and around Wall Township, including several sites along Shark River. These discoveries have helped to substantiate historians' claims of a significant Lenni-Lenape presence in southern Monmouth County during the latter part of the 1600s and into the early 1700s. Even one of Spring Lake Heights' earliest families traced part of their ancestry to an Indian princess in the Lenape tribe.

It is uncertain precisely how many Indians were living in New Jersey when the first wave of European settlers arrived. Some estimates have placed the Native American population at more than thirty-five thousand, while other totals have been much more conservative, at ten to thirteen thousand.

The Lenni-Lenape were a peaceful tribe. Tribal members spent many hours preparing food, clothing and weapons for hunting. As the Indians went about their routine, it is doubtful they had any sense of foreboding about what the ensuing years held in store for them.

Many changes would eventually unfold as European explorers began to cross the Atlantic, thereby ushering in what would become a lengthy period of colonization on the North American shores. By the mid-1700s, very few Lenni-Lenape remained in either Monmouth County or New Jersey.

2

EUROPEAN EXPLORATION AND COLONIZATION

Toward the end of the 1400s, many of the maritime nations of Europe actively sought a shorter passage to the Far East. In 1497, John Cabot and his son Sebastian were among the earliest Europeans to strike out on such a venture, sailing on behalf of the king of England. The initial voyage brought them along the rocky coast of Newfoundland, where it is believed they viewed the coastline without disembarking from the ship. At a later date, Sebastian Cabot made a return trip to North America and sailed along the entire eastern seaboard. From aboard his ship, Cabot claimed all of this territory for the British Crown.

Approximately twenty-five years later, Giovanni de Verrazano, an Italian explorer, sailed for King Francis I of France and found his way to the Monmouth County coastline. Navigating the area along Sandy Hook and Raritan Bay, Verrazano and his crew quickly discovered that this land of steep and wooded hills was not without inhabitants. Scores of Indians gathered along the bayshore to view Verrazano's advancing ship. An encounter between these two parties would have been likely if both the weather and tidal conditions had allowed Verrazano and his crew to make landfall. The explorer was forced to give up further investigation of the area, but not before he laid claim to the entire bayshore region on behalf of the king of France.

More than eighty years passed before the coast of New Jersey was visited by another European explorer. In 1609, an Englishman named Henry Hudson embarked on a journey to find a northwest passage to the Orient. While sailing on behalf of the Dutch East India Company, Hudson discovered New Jersey. He first explored the land around the mouth of the Delaware Bay before traveling north along the coast and continuing into New York Bay.

Hudson's ship, *Half Moon*, dropped anchor off the northern Monmouth County shoreline, where Hudson's crew went ashore and examined some of the land's densely wooded interior. Ultimately, this small expedition marked the first encounter between white men and Native Americans along the New Jersey shore. Unfortunately, the good will that was initially generated between the two parties faded quickly, and one of Hudson's crew members was shot in the throat with an arrow. After further problems with the Indians, Hudson and the remainder of his crew set sail for home.

Approximately a decade later, the Dutch returned to North America and established several settlements and trading posts in areas near New York Bay and Delaware Bay. They also proclaimed the entire mid-Atlantic region "New Netherland."

The discovery of North America generated excitement and interest throughout the cities and ports of Europe. It wasn't long before more European countries became involved in expeditions across the Atlantic.

King Gustavus Adolphus of Sweden granted a charter to the West India Company, whose main purpose was to lay claim to the land around the Delaware River on behalf of Sweden. This claim was made in spite of the fact that both the English and the Dutch had already claimed the same territory.

Upon reaching the shores of the Delaware River, the Swedes sailed a short distance to the north, where they erected a settlement. However, the mighty Norsemen were no match for the masses of mosquitoes that lived in the nearby marshes. Eventually, the Swedes vacated their settlement and moved into other areas of South Jersey, much to the alarm of the Dutch, who resented their encroachment. Under the leadership of Peter Stuyvesant, the Dutch conquered the Swedes and placed them under Dutch rule.

The Dutch's supremacy was short-lived, however, as the English sought to uphold their original claim on North America based on Sebastian Cabot's earlier sightings. The English succeeded in overcoming the Dutch and took full control over their settlements. King Charles II granted the entire region from west of the Connecticut River to the eastern edge of Delaware to his brother, James, the Duke of York.

Colonel Richard Nicolls was placed in charge of the duke's territory, and the colonel rapidly went to work granting tracts of land to English settlers. In a situation where a tract was occupied by a Lenape Indian tribe, the settlers were required to purchase the land from tribal members before taking possession of it. Payment to the Indians was usually made in the form of material goods, such as clothing, gunpowder, tobacco or cider. These payments were quite small, especially when compared to the vast amounts of territory the settlers received in return. Most of the tribal members migrated westward after selling their properties.

In 1664, unbeknownst to Colonel Nicolls, the Duke of York leased the entire area of New Jersey, including its settlers, to two of the duke's closest friends and confidants: John Berkeley, the Baron of Straton, and Sir George Carteret. While both men were given some governmental power over the colony, it was Carteret's young cousin Philip who was appointed to serve as its governor. Berkeley and the elder Carteret called their newly acquired territory "Nova Caesaria," named for the Isle of Jersey, Sir George Carteret's birthplace. In later years, the Latin name was dropped, and the colony was called New Jersey.

Under Governor Philip Carteret's tenure, all of the prior land grants made between Colonel Nicolls and the settlers were nullified, thereby causing many years of squabbling over land rights among the former landholders. Ultimately, all settlers were expected to take out proprietary patents for their lands.

By 1676, New Jersey had been split into two provinces: East Jersey and West Jersey. The boundary line between these provinces extended from a northern point along the Delaware River in current Sussex County and traveled southward to the coast, ending at Little Egg Harbor. For a while, the colony was referred to as "The Jerseys."

Sir George Carteret presided over East Jersey, while West Jersey eventually came under the control of twelve men, one of whom was the renowned Englishman and Quaker William Penn. In time, East Jersey also entered into the hands of Penn, who, along with his associates, formed the General Board of Proprietors. This private company held title to all real estate in the eastern half of the colony on the basis of a release from the estate of Sir George Carteret in 1681. The company was responsible for granting land titles to Jersey's settlers.

Even today, more than three hundred years later, all land titles in eastern New Jersey are obtained from proprietary patents. Titles to disputed or unclaimed property can be received only through the General Board of Proprietors, which is located in Perth Amboy, the original capital of East Jersey.

Despite numerous governmental changes and settlers' indifferences, the colony continued to grow. By 1687, Monmouth Colony had been established.

THE BEGINNING DAYS OF MONMOUTH COUNTY

The earliest settlers in Monmouth County were mostly those of English, Scotch and Irish descent.

In the late 1600s and throughout much of the 1700s, life in the county was less than ideal. In addition to the squabbling that took place regularly between the factions, colonists endured many daily hardships in order to survive. Like the Indians, the settlers preferred to live near rivers or streams, where they had access to water for bathing, washing clothes or travel. Some of the early villages harnessed energy from the various waterways to operate gristmills. Fruits and nuts were gathered from nearby forests and used as regular food supplements. Most settlers were either farmers or fishermen. In later years, a few earned their livelihoods by working for timber companies.

Transportation was quite primitive and was done by boat, horse or on foot. Highways were uneven, and the secondary roads, more often than not, were trails in the woods that were strewn with vines and brambles.

Education and religious instruction were usually conducted in the home, although as areas became more inhabited, small schoolhouses were built to accommodate a particular region's educational needs.

Taverns and inns, usually found along the main highways, provided many of the colonists with their only respite from life's adversities. Townsmen and travelers often gathered at these sites to relax and socialize.

The Revolutionary War period brought an added strain for the colonists, who not only had to defend themselves against the British forces but were also forced to guard against ruthless bands of outlaws who continuously roamed the countryside. These relentless cutthroats resided mostly in swamplands and in areas of dense underbrush, where they could conceal themselves from nearby villages. They brutalized the settlers by night, often stealing from them first before setting fire to the remainder of their properties or even murdering them.

During most of the 1770s, the outlaws operated mainly along the Manasquan River. While they professed to be British Loyalists, many local historians believe the thugs acted strictly for their own gains and not out of an allegiance to the British. By the end of the Revolutionary War period, most attacks on local villages had ceased, and settlers sought to rebuild their lives.

Monmouth County was originally composed of three townships: Freehold Township, Middletown Township and Shrewsbury Township. Its area extended north and west of the Navesink River and south to Little Egg Harbor. The population in the southern part of the county gradually increased as more settlers relocated there from New York, lower New England and other parts of New Jersey. In 1801, Howell Township was created out of Shrewsbury Township, and in 1851, Wall Township became a division of Howell. All of the Jersey Shore towns located between Shark River and the Manasquan River were once part of Wall Township.

3
WALL UNITED METHODIST CHURCH

The 1800s in early America ushered in a period of religious awakening. This movement resulted in revivals among those of the Protestant denominations, especially the Methodists. Prior to this period, there were very few organized churches in southern Monmouth County, and most of the religious training was conducted informally in private homes.

Wall United Methodist Church began humbly in 1834 in a one-room schoolhouse located just north of Wall Road and near a swamp region called Polly Pod Bog. This marsh stretched eastward into Como Lake and contained large amounts of cranberries, which were often gathered by the area's earliest inhabitants.

The schoolhouse, a small log cabin, had been built four years earlier in response to the educational needs of the children who lived in the southeastern section of Wall Township. For the next eighteen years, a small group of residents would meet at the schoolhouse for a preaching service on alternate Wednesday evenings. This service evolved into a society known as the Wall Methodist Episcopal Church.

The little church grew steadily, and by 1846, a Sunday school had been organized. In 1852, the Reverend William Franklin was appointed to serve as the church's first pastor by a senior minister on the Freehold Circuit. The Freehold Circuit was a district that included all of the Methodist Episcopal churches in Monmouth County.

While the new church gained an official pastor, it actually lost its meeting spot when the schoolhouse was moved to New Bedford Corners, presently the site of Wall High School. There, the building was enlarged and transformed into a general store by James Allgor and Jacob Smith. Smith also served as the postmaster for New Bedford. It is doubtful that either Allgor or Smith had ever intended for the church to be without a home.

According to some early accounts, Jacob Smith and his brother Joseph collaborated with Reverend Franklin to have a new church built at the schoolhouse's former site. Jacob Smith's original homestead was located on Old Mill Road, just south of where the church stands today. In the autumn of 1854, Smith and his wife, Elizabeth, deeded a partial acre of land to the Wall Methodist Episcopal Society in the hope that a church would soon be built. In the interim, it is believed the congregation continued to meet for worship in private homes or possibly a local barn or large shed.

Joseph Smith has been credited with helping to design the original church. Through his efforts, and the hard work of numerous others, a new church was erected by the end of the year. Several members of the church referred to the new structure as "a little church on the hill," noting its location, which was at the top of a small incline. The church contained two pot-bellied stoves for heating purposes and a partition that divided the sanctuary and separated the sexes. In addition to the partition, the church also had separate entrances for male and female attendants. This physical separation was a common feature of many churches built during this era. A portion of the property adjacent to the church was designated as a church graveyard.

With Methodism growing increasingly popular, the church expanded its membership. In 1866, thirty-one converts were baptized in Shark River by the church's pastor. Twelve years later, in 1878, the congregation's growth had been substantial enough for the church to appear on an early map of Monmouth County.

The church's rapid development was in marked contrast to a dwindling Presbyterian congregation, which had been meeting since the 1820s in a small cottage located slightly west of the Old Mill Road and Allaire Road intersection. Beset by financial hardship throughout the years, the tiny Presbyterian church shuttered its doors in the early 1870s.

In 1892, the Wall Methodist Episcopal Church was remodeled, at which time the sanctuary's center partition was removed and a single entrance was made at the front of the building. A decade earlier, the church had been named a beneficiary in the will of Mrs. Zilpha Torton, an original member of the Wednesday evening preaching service. Upon Mrs. Torton's death, her home and the land on which the church, Fellowship Hall and the parsonage presently stand became property of the church.

Revival services held here during the latter part of the 1890s were so popular that the minister actually had trouble walking through the crowded sanctuary in his effort to reach the pulpit. By 1899, the church became self-sustaining of the Freehold Circuit, and Reverend Abraham Izzard was appointed the first full-time pastor. The church was incorporated in 1906.

During the next several years, fundraising events such as suppers, festivals and the annual Harvest Home not only helped the church with its regular expenses but also provided the funds for its future remodeling projects. The Harvest Home event was usually attended by several hundred residents, who enjoyed selecting from a wide assortment of produce that was donated to the church by the township's farmers. In 1910, the church building was moved fifty feet to a site that is presently marked by a monument.

Throughout the following decades, additional improvements were made to the building, and the church's trustees were instrumental in forming the Wall Cemetery Improvement Association. The association consisted of both church officials and plot owners who were committed to the perpetual care of the cemetery. Several of the church's original trustees are buried in this cemetery, including brothers Jacob and Joseph Smith.

A general merger between the Methodist Episcopal and the Methodist Protestant denominations took place in 1939, at which time the church adopted its new official name: Wall Methodist Church.

In 1955, the men of the church led a drive to construct a new social hall. The old building that they sought to replace was originally a stable for the minister's horse and had been later converted for use as a meeting spot. Through the generous financial support of the members and the efforts of the men who volunteered their labor, a new Fellowship Hall became a reality later that year.

During the same decade, attendance at the summer Bible School and at the regular Sunday service increased significantly. Within a short period of time, members realized that facilities at the church were no longer adequate, and a larger building was needed.

Envisioning a bigger church, volunteers cleared a wooded area at the eastern edge of the property, where they relocated the parsonage and the garage. By December 1961, ground had been broken for the construction of a new sanctuary, nearer to Old Mill Road. After eleven months of hard and dedicated work, the building was completed, and members held their first worship service in the new church.

The front entrance of Wall United Methodist Church on Old Mill Road. The current sanctuary was constructed in 1962. *Courtesy of the author.*

While the congregation appreciated the more spacious and modern accommodations, they still cherished their old church and planned to use it for Sunday school and other educational activities. Sadly, those particular plans were never implemented. During the nighttime hours of December 31, 1962, a quick-moving fire ravaged the old church, leaving only the foundation and parts of the north and south walls standing. The fire had started in the basement near the furnace. Seventy-five volunteer firefighters from four different fire companies braved frigid temperatures and a biting windchill to battle the blaze. Unfortunately, their valiant attempt to save the 108-year-old structure was futile.

Firemen remained at the scene until the following afternoon, while members and residents gaped in disbelief at the smoldering ruins. One church member and former resident of Wall Road remembers returning to the site several days later to collect fragments from the building's broken stained-glass windows. She had wanted a keepsake from the beloved old church.

Once recovered from the initial shock of the fire, the congregation moved forward. In addition to starting a small lending library, members also replaced numerous Bibles, choir robes and music sheets that had been lost in the blaze. An iron bell, salvaged from the building's charred ruins, was later made into a monument and placed at the site of where the former church had once stood.

By February 1965, plans had been formulated for a new educational building, and the congregation celebrated the end of a substantial mortgage that had been taken out for the new sanctuary and for the moving and renovation of the parsonage.

Throughout the years, the church has played an important role in the community, offering numerous outreach programs to its neighbors. Some of these programs and activities have included movies that were presented in Fellowship Hall, lively costume parties at Halloween and even afternoon typing lessons for students who felt they needed to improve on their typing skills. In the late 1970s, summer evening worship services for the community were held in a field behind the church building.

The ladies of the church have maintained a very active role here and have coordinated countless events, such as covered-dish suppers

A bell monument marks the site where the original Wall Methodist Church stood before it was destroyed by fire in 1962. *Courtesy of the author.*

and the annual Blueberry Festival, a local favorite. During national wartime, they have provided letters and packages of cookies to those of the congregation who were serving in the military.

The church's building is home to a successful child-care center. While the center operates independently of the church, a member of the congregation is credited with having been the center's original founder.

As in times past, the church continues to thrive. The clergy and members extend warmth and caring similar to the feelings shared by the congregation of more than a century ago, when the Wall Methodist Episcopal Church was fondly referred to as "a little church on the hill."

4

VILLA PARK

The southern portion of Spring Lake Heights, which includes the natural beauty of Wreck Pond, Black Creek and the Old Mill Pond and Stream, was known in its earlier days as Villa Park. While small businesses and attractive neighborhoods dot the current landscape, the presence of these waterways, with their banks encased in lush flora and sea grasses, have helped to lend an almost semi-rural aspect to certain blocks of this area.

In 1708, Thomas Tilton purchased land north of Wreck Pond from James Grover. Grover was a resident and businessman from Middletown who was one of the original landholders under the Monmouth Patent. In 1716, George Rodgers bought an adjoining section of land north and west of the Tilton property from William Brindley. In the following years, another member of the Rodgers family, Benjamin Rodgers, acquired additional properties in the area, including the land along the south side of Wreck Pond.

For most of the 1600s, the Lenni-Lenape Indians occupied parts of this territory. Eventually, proprietors of a landholding company from northern Monmouth County purchased the land from the Indians.

In 1801, the Rodgers family consolidated their properties around Black Creek and created Rodgers Park. This area consisted mostly of woods, farmlands and orchards.

The Wreck Pond shoreline. Pictured here are gourds that serve as birdhouses for nesting purple martins. *Courtesy of the author.*

The Squan Turnpike, currently known as State Highway 71, was a privately financed toll road that ran through Villa Park and continued northward into other sections of Wall Township. Many years later, the turnpike would become a state-owned road.

In 1802, a post office was established at the corner of the Squan Turnpike and Prospect Avenue, where Jerome Allen served as the area's first postmaster. Upon Allen's death, his wife assumed the role of postmistress. Future generations of the Allen family resided in the general vicinity. During much of the 1900s, the family owned a vegetable farm at the northwest corner of the state highway and Prospect Avenue. PNC Bank now occupies the site.

The post office continued to operate until approximately 1940, when it was closed due to the start of home mail delivery.

While much of southern Monmouth County experienced a modest but steady growth throughout the 1800s, the thrust of development and population growth in Villa Park did not take place until the 1870s. This expansion was due largely to the entrepreneurial efforts of two ambitious businessmen, John Rodgers and William Reid, both of whom were stagecoach owners. Up until this period, the stagecoach industry in America had thrived, as "coaches" were widely used for transporting passengers and freight. However, with the emergence of the railroad, the era of the stagecoach was in a rapid decline. Apart from utilizing the smaller coach services for local needs, Americans now preferred to do their distance traveling by sea or rail.

Both Rodgers and Reid responded to the downward trend in their industry by embarking on a new business venture. In 1875, Reid purchased the portion of land located south of Rodgers's property, subdivided it and constructed summer cottages there. The cottages were either sold or rented to prominent vacationers from New York and Philadelphia. Reid called his resort area Villa Park. The tourist industry was not altogether new to Reid, who had been partially responsible for developing the resort town of Brighton a few years earlier. Brighton later became part of Spring Lake. Around this same period, Rodgers converted his landholdings into a neighboring resort.

The success enjoyed by both Rodgers and Reid was due in large part to the arrival of the railroad at the Jersey Shore. By 1875, railroad service between Long Branch and Belmar had been established. Passengers who wished to travel to points farther south were taken to their destinations by stagecoach. Approximately a decade later, train service was extended to Bay Head. The popularity of the railroad helped to increase tourism and a year-round population at the coast. William Reid especially benefited from the railroad's expansion.

When the country's Centennial Exposition in Philadelphia closed in the autumn of 1876, many of the exposition's buildings were sold, dismantled and shipped to various locations throughout the country. Two of these buildings—the Missouri State Building and the New Hampshire State Building—were sold to two different purchasers from New York and shipped by train to Spring Lake. A year later, both buildings were reassembled on lots located near Wreck Pond in Villa Park. Additional lumber from former buildings in the exposition was purchased and used to erect barns and fences in Villa Park.

By the mid-1870s, Rodgers and Reid had won approval from the state for the construction of a public road that would travel from the Squan Turnpike to the ocean. This course would provide summer vacationers with easier access to the beach. Once completed, the road, which is currently known as Ocean Road, divided the two resorts into Rodgers's Villa Park to the north and Reid's Villa Park to the south. Eventually, Rodgers sold his portion of real estate to Reid, and in 1888, the two areas became one.

When the Borough of Spring Lake was incorporated in 1892, the section of Villa Park that was located east of the railroad became a part of Spring Lake. In 1900, Villa Park still encompassed a sizable region that ran from the upper branch of Black Creek south to Wreck Pond and extended west to the area located around the Old Mill Pond and Stream. A blacksmith shop opened near the corner of Eighth Avenue and Ocean Road, followed by a few other small grocers located closer to the Squan Turnpike. As more residents settled into southern Monmouth County, Villa Park's population increased enough to warrant a school.

THE VILLA PARK SCHOOL

In 1905, a small school was erected at the corner of Ocean Road and Ninth Avenue. The school consisted of one large room with a partition that divided the room into two sections. These sections were named the West Room and the East Room. Kindergarten through fifth-grade students attended this school, while students in the sixth through eighth grades completed their elementary school education at the bigger Como Grammar School.

The Villa Park School was closed after the Spring Lake Heights Elementary School opened in 1938. The Cornelius V. Kelly Community Center now stands at the school's former site.

The Cornelius V. Kelly Community Center on Ocean Road. *Courtesy of the author.*

The Villa Park Chapel

The cornerstone for the Villa Park Chapel was laid on Ocean Road in 1920, and the first formal services were held there in 1924.

The chapel actually had its beginning three years earlier in 1917, when two members of St. Andrew's Methodist Church in Spring Lake started Sunday school classes for the children of Villa Park. Anna Dodd and Anna Scott, both of whom were Villa Park residents, felt there was a great need for religious education there. At the time, the nearest church was located in Lake Como, and Dodd and Scott lobbied hard for the construction of a church closer to their area. These ladies were joined in their efforts by the pastor of St. Andrew's Church and a friend from its congregation, Lena Williams.

The Villa Park Chapel held regular services until 1954, when its members agreed to a merger with Como Methodist Church, located in the north end of town. The chapel was eventually sold and converted into a private residence.

WILLIAM REID'S LODGE

In approximately 1875, William Reid built a lodging house and general store at the corner of the turnpike and Ocean Road. Included within this building was a small eatery for the lodge's guests and other tourists who had come to vacation at Reid's new resort. Throughout the years, a restaurant was operated there at various times. A few of the borough's longtime residents recalled the summers of the 1930s and '40s, when seasonal visitors dined alfresco at attractive tables on the lodge's front porch. A red, white and blue bunting was often draped over the porch's railing.

In 1927, it was here, in the lobby of Reid's former hostelry, where the residents of Villa Park and Lake Como cast their ballots and decided to incorporate their two areas into the Borough of Spring Lake Heights.

For most of the 1900s, the lodge was known as the Newark House. More recently, this historic landmark underwent an extensive refurbishment and currently serves as the Evergreen Inn, a popular bed-and-breakfast.

The historic Evergreen Inn graces the corner of State Highway 71 and Ocean Road. The inn was originally built as a general store and lodge in 1875. *Courtesy of the author.*

5
A SEA CAPTAIN'S CHURCH

Sea Plain

By the 1870s, much of the southern Monmouth County area was inhabited by either fishermen or farmers. The portion of Spring Lake Heights north of St. Clair Avenue that included the vicinity around Wall Road was known as Sea Plain. For a time, this area was also referred to as "Pearce's," named for James Pearce, a local landowner.

Sea Plain was a small village situated on the west side of the New York and Long Branch Railroad line. The village contained a general store owned by the Pearce family and a schoolhouse that was attended by many of the township's children. In 1873, a post office was established near the corner of the turnpike and Allaire Road, where Jack Pearce served as postmaster.

There were no churches in Sea Plain up until this period. However, this situation was destined to change, due in large part to the concern and generosity of another local landowner.

The Methodist Church of Sea Plain

Samuel Ludlow was a wealthy sea captain who resided on a farm in nearby Spring Lake. While Captain Ludlow was a man of deep

Como Methodist Church, circa 1930s. Captain Samuel Ludlow donated the funds and land for its construction in the early 1870s. *Courtesy of John Miller.*

religious convictions, he seldom attended church for the simple reason that few churches existed in his immediate area.

Aside from the Wall Methodist Church, there was only a handful of other churches scattered throughout the southern part of Wall Township. Individuals and families who wanted to attend Sunday services either walked or rode great distances in horse-drawn wagons on narrow paths or irregular roads in order to reach a particular church.

In 1861, Ludlow and his family trekked to Wall Methodist Church after his wife, Sarah, died. Following her funeral service at the church, her body was brought back to the family farm for burial. The ordeal further strengthened Ludlow's resolve to establish a church locally.

By the latter part of the decade, he had cleared one of his properties, located at the lower end of Como-Allaire Road, which is now Church Street. He donated the land, along with a substantial sum of money, for the construction of a church. In addition to Ludlow, organizers of the project included Ludlow's new wife, Nancy; James Allgor; Phoebe Newman; and Jonathan Brown.

By 1872, the Methodist Church of Sea Plain was nearly completed. The new church was quite small and contained a large stove in the center of a single room, around which the congregation gathered for worship. A portion of land just west of the building was set aside for a village graveyard. The back end of this property was designated a burial ground for the bodies of shipwrecked sailors that washed ashore on local beaches.

In Ludlow's original deed to the church, he prohibited the use of any musical instruments inside the church building. He especially disapproved of the violin, believing it to be an instrument of the devil.

The Reverend E.D. Stulz served as the church's first preacher until 1878, when he was succeeded by his son, the Reverend L.D. Stulz. In 1887, after Sea Plain had been renamed Lake Como, the church's formal name was changed to Como Methodist Protestant Church.

As new families and businesses moved into the village, the church's membership expanded. By the time the Reverend J.C. Austerberry had arrived as the new pastor in 1897, a building committee was formulating plans to enlarge the church. Renovations were completed in the summer of 1898, and a parsonage was built adjacent to the church. An Adult Fellowship and a Ladies' Aid Society were instrumental in raising funds and assisting the church with its forward progress.

During these years, the church published a bulletin entitled *Our Caller*. In addition to announcements regarding church activities, the small publication also contained written commentary by the clergy and congregation. *Our Caller* was especially popular with merchants from Lake Como and Spring Lake, who used the publication to advertise their businesses.

Before his death in 1901, Samuel Ludlow had joyfully witnessed the steady growth of the church, which had fully evolved from a handful of worshippers thirty years earlier. Throughout the early part of the century, members continued to upgrade the building, which included the conversion of the church's basement into a room for a Sunday school.

In 1939, the church officially adopted a new name: Como Methodist Church. The following year, a special program was launched to pay off a longstanding mortgage on the church over a three-year period. This goal was accomplished in spite of the difficult economic times and the country's entry into World War II. The mortgage was burned in 1944.

Four years later, a committee was appointed to care for the cemetery, which by now had become the burial site for Samuel Ludlow and members of his family, several of whom were military veterans.

The 1950s ushered in another period of growth for the church. Its social activities, which had decreased during the war, now resumed at a full pace. Covered-dish suppers, Christmas pageants and the annual Harvest Home Dinner were popular events. A quilting bee met weekly at the church. One former member happily recalled climbing up to the church's bell tower each Sunday, where he proudly tolled the bell before the weekly worship service. Like many other children from town, he also attended the church's Vacation Bible School each summer.

In 1954, the church merged with the Villa Park Methodist Church from the south end of the borough. Once the merger was completed, the congregation adopted its official new name: Christ Methodist Church. The former Villa Park Church building was sold to a family and converted into a private residence.

In June 1960, members of Christ Methodist Church approved a merger that would make them a part of St. Andrew's Methodist Church in Spring Lake. Christ Church's congregation now met in Spring Lake for worship and other related activities. For the trustees of St. Andrew's Methodist Church, the dilemma of how to dispose of Christ Church's former site was resolved when the building was purchased by the Craftsman's Club of Manasquan. The Craftsman's Club served as an adjunct to the Spring Lake–Wall Masonic Lodge. Their newly acquired building would provide lodge members with a future meeting place.

The Ocean Lodge

Currently, this former church is home to the Ocean Lodge, an organization of Freemasons. The group is composed of 150 members who reside throughout the Jersey Shore area. The Freemasons are an extraordinary association of men who work diligently to help support the local families in need, in addition to aiding organizations such as hospitals and food banks. During the summer of 2010, the lodge received an extensive renovation of its interior, at which time the walls, floors and ceilings were completely refurbished.

The former Como Church is currently home to the Ocean Lodge, an organization of Freemasons. Captain Ludlow's grave is marked by the tall white monument next door. *Courtesy of the author.*

An interior view of the Masonic Lodge in 2011 reveals several of the original stained-glass windows from the Como Methodist Church. *Courtesy of the author.*

One of the organization's members, a local contractor, donated much of his time and talent to the project, which helped to further enhance the lodge's historic charm. Many of the building's original features, including its nooks, stairwells, vestibule and several small windows of stained glass, serve as reminders of a much earlier period. The lodge's main room contains the heavy wooden pews that once belonged to the sanctuary of Como Methodist Church. After more than 130 years, this historic structure continues to serve as a meeting spot for those who have dedicated themselves to the service of helping others.

6
THE VILLAGE OF LAKE COMO

In 1880, a large land purchase by two local businessmen, Henry Yard and William "Silas" Force, combined the village of Sea Plain with a small area of land named Kitchentown. Kitchentown ran north of Brighton Avenue to St. Clair Avenue. It also included the land that bordered Beverly Avenue. Yard and Force named their village Lake Como after a city of the same name in Italy.

Soon after the village had been established, a schoolhouse was built across from the Como Methodist Church. The structure was a reddish one-room log cabin with a fireplace. Occasionally, a snake appeared in one of the schoolroom's dark corners, much to the horror of the teacher and pupils. The school was attended by approximately 130 students who lived in and around the Lake Como vicinity. The schoolhouse was later purchased by Henry Yard, who moved the building to Pitney Avenue in Spring Lake.

Como Grammar School

In 1883, a larger school was built in a wooded area along what is now State Highway 71, between St. Clair Avenue and Ludlow

Above: The former Como Grammar School as it appeared in the 1800s. The school operated for fifty-five years until the Spring Lake Heights Elementary School opened in 1938. *Courtesy of the Veltre family.*

Opposite: An eighth-grade class poses for a graduation portrait on the steps of the Como Grammar School, circa 1910. *Courtesy of the Veltre family.*

Avenue. The new school, named Como Grammar School, consisted of two stories and contained two rooms on both the first and second floors. Each room had a partition that could be used when it became necessary to divide the classes. The school was attended by students up through the eighth grade. George Allard, a Civil War veteran, was the school's first teacher. At a later period, Dr. H.W. Mountz, a renowned local educator, also served as principal there for a short interval.

The Como Grammar School remained in operation until 1938, when the borough built an elementary school on the corner of Brighton Avenue and the highway. The Como school building stood vacant for several years before it was destroyed by fire. A couple homes now occupy the school's former site.

The Como Station

By the early 1880s, many parts of the Jersey Shore had seen an increase in tourism and a year-round population. This was especially true of the Spring Lake area, where wealthy businessmen and landowners purchased additional properties for development. Lands located to the east of Lake Como were a prime example of this trend. Judge John Remsen and Captain Pitney Curtis were two among several local land developers who divided their properties into building lots.

In response to this building trend, Henry Yard sought to accommodate visitors and prospective real estate clients by upgrading the area's transportation needs. In 1883, Yard, with some assistance from his wife, designed and built an attractive stone railroad station near the tracks opposite Lake Como. The new Como Station stood at the foot of South Boulevard and Fourth Avenue in Spring Lake. Passengers who disembarked from the trains were met by waiting stagecoaches that transported them

Above: The Como Railroad Station was built in 1883 by developer Henry Yard and serviced Lake Como and its surrounding area for a half century. *Courtesy of John Miller.*

Below: A locomotive pulls into the Como Railroad Station in 1908. *Courtesy of the Wickham family.*

to their desired locations. Several decades later, students from Lake Como and the surrounding area utilized the station and rail service when traveling to their classes at either Manasquan High School or Asbury Park High School.

In addition to passenger service, the Como Station also provided shipping from a loading dock at the south end of the station. This service was a great convenience for local residents and tourists, who had previously taken their parcels to Keansburg, where they were eventually shipped to a distribution center in New York City.

By the end of the 1920s, the increasing popularity of the automobile and town trolley services caused an overall decline in train ridership at the shore. The Spring Lake railroad station, located a short distance away, adequately supplied the local area's need for a railroad depot. After a half century of service, the Como Station was demolished in 1934.

The Kilo Factory

The historic brick building located at Railroad Avenue and Wall Road was constructed in 1888 for the purpose of supplying electricity to Lake Como and Spring Lake. In the early 1920s, the building was known as the Kilo Factory, named for the French measurement. During World War II, it served as an armory. Following the end of the war, the building was converted into a factory that made metallic threads for textile mills. This factory was succeeded by another plant that manufactured rubber coats and boots. Recreational basketball games were played there during the 1950s and drew a considerable number of area participants.

The building stood mostly vacant for more than a decade before its interior was remodeled and transformed into office space by a local realtor. More recently, the former Kilo Factory served as home to a preschool.

EGGIMANN'S TAVERN

In 1884, local businessman Walter Eggimann opened the Lake Como Hotel, located between his home and a brewery business he owned on the Squan Turnpike in Lake Como. While beer and other liquors were bottled at his plant, the hotel served as a regular stagecoach stop for numerous travelers on the turnpike. Upon Eggimann's death nearly thirty years later, his son William closed the brewery and converted the hotel into Eggimann's Tavern. For more than forty years, the tavern remained one of the town's favorite gathering spots for food and spirits. The restaurant's home-baked clam pies were among its most popular dishes.

When the Ferrette family purchased the tavern from the Eggimanns in 1957, they made only a few minor alterations to the building's interior. The new owners instead chose to focus on continuing the tavern's tradition of good food and added new items to the menu. The restaurant's hamburger, served on two slices of white bread, was as popular a feature as the Eggimanns' clam pie had been.

Wagons pulled by teams of horses were common sights on the Squan Turnpike, now Route 71. *Courtesy of the Wickham family.*

From 1980 until 2006, the tavern was owned and operated by the Kolarsick family, who maintained the restaurant's quality fare.

Today, the former stagecoach stop and tavern is home to St. Stephen's Green, an attractive Irish pub.

7
EARLY PERSONALITIES

THE SAMUEL LUDLOW FAMILY

Samuel Ludlow was born in July 1822 to James and Nancy Ludlow. His father, James, was from Bergen County, New Jersey, while his mother, the former Nancy Lee, was born and raised in coastal Virginia.

Although James Ludlow had three sisters and five brothers, it was he who was elected to oversee his father's will when the senior Ludlow died, leaving behind a sizable fortune. A part of this estate included fishing rights in the Hudson River, which were bequeathed to James. At James's death, these fishing rights were inherited by his son Samuel, who operated a shad fishery there for several decades.

Through the success of the fishery, Ludlow amassed great wealth, a part of which he later invested into real estate and other business interests. These businesses included a coastal fishing vessel and a brickyard. He was known to his contemporaries as "Captain" Ludlow.

In June 1848, he married Sarah Smith, the daughter of Jacob Smith, a Wall Township businessman and landowner. Theirs was a happy marriage that produced six children. Sadly, the marriage ended with Sarah's death thirteen years later.

Prior to his wife's passing, Ludlow had acquired vast amounts of farmland throughout the northern areas of Spring Lake and Spring Lake Heights from his father-in-law. The Ludlow farm consisted of one hundred acres, which extended from the ocean to the Squan Turnpike and included property located between today's Worthington Avenue and Monroe Avenue in Spring Lake. Ludlow also owned a smaller section of land between Worthington Avenue and his home at the corner of Tuttle and Fourth Avenues in Spring Lake.

The sea captain made a wholehearted attempt at farming but found much of the farm's soil too sandy and of poor quality to produce very much. Ludlow raised and sold turkeys for a few years before he eventually sold the farm to the Tuttle family. Ultimately, the Tuttles divided the land into streets and building lots.

The sale of this property made the Ludlows one of the wealthiest families in Monmouth County. At the time of the sale, Ludlow was remarried, and he and his second wife, Nancy, had added nine new children to their family. In addition to rearing fifteen children and tending to his business interests, Ludlow also served as keeper of the United States Life-Saving Station at Spring Lake. The U.S. Life-Saving Service was a forerunner of today's U.S. Coast Guard.

In the early 1870s, he and his wife organized plans for the construction of a new church in the neighboring village of Sea Plain. Throughout the years, Ludlow and his family were renowned for their many acts of kindness toward the poor. No one was ever turned away from enjoying a meal at the family's dinner table.

When Captain Ludlow passed away in 1901, Como Church could not hold the amount of local residents and business associates who came to pay their respects to him. His body was laid to rest in the Como Church cemetery, where a tall white monument currently marks his burial site. More than eighty years later, a local family purchased Ludlow's former farmhouse in Spring Lake and moved the home to a nearby location in Spring Lake Heights.

Jonathan Brown Jr.

Jonathan Brown Jr. was a hardworking and pious man who was greatly admired for his acts of charity toward the area's impoverished widows and children. He was also known for running his household with an iron fist. Jonathan's stern personality was in marked contrast to that of his wife, Mary, a vivacious raven-haired beauty who was full of fun.

Throughout his life, Jonathan had maintained his family's proud tradition in farming. His grandfather, Elihau Brown, had been among the first wave of English settlers who arrived at the Jersey Shore in the 1700s. Elihau Brown had received a grant of land from the king of England that consisted of eight hundred acres of choice but irregularly shaped inland property. This property stretched from an area west of Como Lake, south to the present-day corner of Morris Avenue and Fifth Avenue in Spring Lake. The

The former Brown-Wickham Homestead stood near the corner of Allaire Road and Highway 71 until the property was sold to a developer in 1971. Town houses now occupy the site. *Courtesy of Jean Worthington.*

property continued farther south to include land that bordered the Manasquan River.

Possessing such a large territory in what was later to become Spring Lake Heights led some local historians to christen Elihau Brown with the nickname the "Great-Great-Granddaddy of Spring Lake Heights."

While portions of the family's territory were gradually sold off, the Browns still retained a sizable amount of farmland. The Brown farmhouse, or plantation, was located on the lower end of Allaire Road and was built of wood from storm-battered ships that had washed ashore along local beaches.

In the early and mid-1800s, Jonathan Brown Jr. was a major farmer who regularly sold vast amounts of produce to individual families and businesses. He routinely directed a team of wagons to Keyport, where he helped to unload his produce onto barges that transported the cargo to markets in New York City. At the height of the growing season, his youngest son, Adam, sold produce to residents and businesses in Belmar.

Brown had five children, and as a parent, he was very strict. His son Joseph was quite similar to his wife, Mary—good-looking and full of personality. Ultimately, Joseph's fondness for people and parties not only placed him at odds with Jonathan but also helped to cast his future.

JOSEPH BROWN

Joseph was fully aware that his father did not approve of any form of frolicking. However, he was willing to risk the unpleasant consequences when he slipped out of the house on Saturday nights to regularly attend the weekly dances at Our House Tavern in Farmingdale.

Jonathan Brown, who firmly believed that the music played in taverns would lead folks on a clear path to hell, was livid whenever he learned of Joseph's misbehavior. This disobedience always resulted in Joseph being ordered to the barn for a horsewhipping.

Joseph's brother Abbott also suffered the same consequences for his misdeeds.

Fearful of future whippings, Joseph and Abbot conspired to run away, but not before they tucked a farewell note for their mother underneath a sack of cornmeal in the pantry. The two teenagers went to sea as cabin boys with Captain Boudish, a local sea captain. Joseph and Abbott made two voyages to Europe before Abbott decided to settle in California. Sadly for Joseph, his brother never returned to New Jersey.

Joseph did return home between voyages and finished his education at a schoolhouse in New Bedford. While at sea, Joseph proved himself to be a very able-bodied seaman. When Captain Boudish's son-in-law, Captain James Craig, received his first command, Joseph traveled aboard Craig's masted sailing ship as a sailing master. The rank was equivalent to the position of first lieutenant. Joseph was only twenty years old. For the next twenty years, he sailed from New York to various European ports, distributing assorted cargoes.

Blanche Blades Brown proudly sits in Joseph Braun's Maxwell in 1913. Joseph Braun was fond of cars and owned one of the first automobiles in Monmouth County. *Courtesy of Jean Worthington.*

Left: Joseph Edgar Brown visits his father's fishery in Mantoloking about 1916. *Courtesy of Jean Worthington.*

Below: Joseph Brown (center) is joined by friends from Lake Como at the Spring Lake beach. *Courtesy of Jean Worthington.*

In December 1877, Joseph married pretty Lucinda Allgor, a native of Wall Township and the great-granddaughter of Nathan Campbell, an officer of the Revolutionary War. The couple resided in the Brown family's homestead on Allaire Road. Joseph resigned his position as sailing master in order to be closer to his wife and their growing family. Their marriage produced a total of seven children, two of whom died at a very young age.

Next to his family, Joseph's greatest love was still the sea.

He became a member of Life-Saving Station No. 8 in Spring Lake, where he assisted with many shipwrecks along the coast. A few years later, he joined with his cousin Wolcott as a proprietor in five fishponds, two in Bay Head and three in Mantaloking. Joseph fancied automobiles and owned one of the first cars in Monmouth County.

Although Joseph had always helped his family and those who were in need, it was in his retirement that he made perhaps the biggest contribution to his community. In the early 1920s, Spring Lake Heights, then Lake Como, did not have its own water system.

When Joseph wanted to install a modern bathroom at his farmhouse, he first obtained permission from the Borough of Spring Lake to connect a pipe into the town's water system. Joseph made this connection a block away from his home, where he placed the main water meter near the railroad tracks. Thinking of his neighbors, he took the situation a step further and installed a pipe big enough to supply all of Lake Como with water. Joseph then placed individual meters in the homes that connected with his water system and collected the necessary fees. Many residents throughout Lake Como benefitted from Joseph Brown's ingenuity.

J. Edgar Brown

Joseph Edgar Brown, the eldest son of Joseph Brown, opened a gas station across from the Brown Homestead at the corner of Allaire Road and State Highway 71. The station was located at the former site of a blacksmith shop previously owned by Elons Garthwaite.

In 1922, J. Edgar built a gas station at the southeast corner of Ludlow Avenue and the highway, where he sold gasoline from three prominent companies: Texaco, Sun and Standard Oil. When J. Edgar had a major disagreement with two of the companies, Sun and Standard Oil, he asked them to remove their gasoline tanks from his property. Both of the companies responded angrily and threatened to put the station out of business. However, the threat never materialized, and J. Edgar enjoyed a long and successful relationship with the Texaco Company.

When J. Edgar died in 1953, his son, Edgar "Ned" Brown, and Ned's son-in-law, Lee Francis, continued to operate the business for the next thirty years. Today, JMA Auto Service occupies the site.

Martha Brown Wickham

The daughter of Joseph Brown, Martha was a woman of indomitable spirit who blazed a trail locally like few others before her.

Martha was a graduate of the Como Grammar School and Chattle High School in Long Branch. She married Claude Wickham, a local businessman, and gave birth to the couple's only child, a son, Jay, in 1907. The marriage ended in divorce several years later.

In 1916, Martha charted a new course and enrolled in studies at the Trenton Normal School, where she graduated with a degree in domestic sciences two years later. She was thirty-seven years old.

Martha taught at the West Belmar Elementary School in Wall Township before she assumed the position of home economics teacher at Manasquan High School. She furthered her education by obtaining a bachelor's of science degree in education from Rutgers University and, later, pursued postgraduate work at Columbia University in New York.

In the summer of 1934, Martha surprised her family and the community when she joined Florence Hale's Alaskan Adventurers for an informational tour of the Alaskan frontier. Martha was only one of two educators from New Jersey to have made this unique trip.

Martha Wickham, a borough resident and teacher, joined a group of educators from across the country for an Alaskan Adventure in July 1934. Martha is pictured third from the left. *Courtesy of the Wickham family.*

Widely admired for her accomplishments in education, Martha was also known for her involvement in local politics. In 1927, she helped in spearheading the drive to have Spring Lake Heights incorporated as a borough. Nearly forty years later, Martha actively campaigned for the election of James Howard, a local schoolteacher who succeeded in his bid to become a representative in the United States Congress.

Rebecca and Charles Worthington

When ten-year-old Rebecca "Rae" Coleman disembarked from a train in Long Branch in 1896, little did she realize that her life was about to undergo a dramatic transformation.

Rae had been one of five siblings placed in a New York City orphanage operated by the American Female Guardian Society. Rae's mother had succumbed to tuberculosis, and her father had died shortly thereafter. Each summer, the children of this city orphanage were brought by train to a summer orphanage in Long Branch, where the public was given the opportunity to meet the youngsters. Those who were living along the shore and who attended this meeting determined which of the youngsters were suitable to perform domestic work in their homes.

Allan and Susan Wickham were among those who had come to the orphanage in the summer of 1896. Upon being introduced to Rae, the couple was quite impressed with the sweet and soft-spoken young girl. The Wickhams, more than wanting Rae to assist them with housekeeping, decided to bring her back to Lake Como, where they would finish raising her. Rae was treated well but worked hard at helping to prepare the meals for Allan's employees. She also pitched in with numerous chores at Allan's general store.

After her arrival in Lake Como, Rae displayed precociousness in music. She was given piano lessons, which further developed her ability, and several years later, she was playing organ at Como Methodist Church. Recognizing the girl's burgeoning talent, Allan and Susan wanted to send her to New York for further musical instruction. However, fate intervened when Rae met and fell in love with Charles Worthington, a member of the Como Methodist Church. Rae and Charles were married there in 1906.

Charles Worthington had been one of twelve children born into a family that traced its roots to sixteenth-century England. Prior to their arrival in New Jersey, the Worthingtons had first settled in Pennsylvania after receiving a land grant from Governor William Penn in the 1700s. Locally, Charles Worthington was an accomplished carpenter who was employed by H.H. Moore, an acclaimed builder whose works included numerous homes, hotels and the former Martin Maloney estate in Spring Lake.

In 1922, Charles Worthington built a home for his beloved wife and family at the lower end of Wall Road. He labored on the project for three years, working on weekends and nights by the light of a kerosene lamp. Roderick Allgor, a local tradesman, performed all of the plastering work at the site. The home still remains in the Worthington family.

Allan D. Wickham

Family records are unclear as to exactly when Allan Wickham first came to Lake Como. His family had originally settled in the foothills of the Catskill Mountains in southeast New York.

Allan had an extensive education. He was awarded a diploma from the Eastman National Business College in Poughkeepsie in 1874. Four years later, he graduated from the New York State Normal School in Albany, where he earned his credentials for teaching. Both degrees served him well.

After graduation, Allan taught at a school near Oneonta, New York. He also served as a traveling teacher, riding on horseback to the individual homes of children who lived in the more isolated regions of the mountains. In Lake Como, Allan taught at the Como Grammar School for a part of the 1880s, before deciding to open a general store at the junction of Church Street and the Squan Turnpike.

In the late 1890s, Allan was appointed to the position of postmaster for Lake Como, a move that proved quite lucrative for his business. Residents who stopped by the store to check their postal boxes very often shopped for groceries and household products as well. Some of Allan's steadiest customers were wealthy matrons from the north end of Spring Lake who regularly dispatched members of their household staffs to shop at his store.

During the busy summer months, Allan also sold various amounts of produce to local hotel kitchens. The store's main counter contained jars of penny candies that were popular with children and adults alike.

On many cold winter nights, Allan's store was a familiar gathering spot for the "Hot Stove League," a group of neighborhood men who enjoyed conversing while seated around the store's coal-burning stove.

Allan Wickham feeds chickens at his property in 1924. Up until the 1940s, many homeowners in town raised chickens for personal consumption. *Courtesy of the Wickham family.*

A. D. WICKHAM & SON,

DEALERS IN

COAL AND WOOD,

HAY, STRAW, GRAIN, ETC.,

OFFICE, THIRD AVENUE, OPPOSITE SMITH'S STABLES,

SPRING LAKE, N. J.

YARD AND STORE-HOUSE LUDLOW AVE. WEST OF R. R.

'PHONE 38 W

Allan Wickham was joined by his son, Claude, in the family's coal, hay and grain business. *Courtesy of the Wickham family.*

Left: Susan Ludlow Wickham was the youngest daughter of Samuel and Sarah Ludlow and wife of Allan Wickham. Susan often entertained and was considered a skilled hostess. *Courtesy of the Wickham family.*

Below: A side view of the home built by Alan and Susan Wickham on Church Street in 1901. *Courtesy of the Wickham family.*

Allan was married to Susan Ludlow, the daughter of Sarah and Captain Samuel Ludlow. They enjoyed a long and happy marriage, which produced a son, Claude. Susan was considered a very cordial hostess who entertained often for friends and her husband's business associates.

In addition to the general store, Allan also operated a successful coal, hay and grain business near the railroad on Ludlow Avenue in Lake Como.

While the wholesale end of the business was conducted in Lake Como, a separate retail office was maintained at the corner of

Morris and Third Avenues in Spring Lake, where clients placed their orders. Eventually, Claude joined the business.

In 1901, Allan and Susan built a large farmhouse by the Como Methodist Church on property that previously had belonged to Susan's father. Their home was later remodeled. In 1927, Allan was elected to serve as one of the borough's first councilmen.

NATHANIEL STONE

During the early 1900s, a large and attractive Victorian-style residence stood on the west side of the Squan Turnpike in Villa Park. This three-story home belonged to local businessman Nathaniel Stone. Stone owned and operated a highly successful produce enterprise that bore his name: Nathaniel Stone and Company. While the business was based in Asbury Park, Stone's company made regular deliveries to hotels and restaurants throughout the coastal area. The Berkeley Carteret Hotel in Asbury Park and the Monmouth Hotel in Spring Lake were two of the company's biggest accounts.

Nathaniel Stone and his family enjoyed relaxing on the front porch of their home located on the state highway. Stone's former home is now the Spring Lake Manor. *Courtesy of the Veltre family.*

After the crash of the stock market and the onset of the Great Depression in 1929, Nathanial Stone's business folded. Similar to countless other Americans during this period, Stone lost nearly all of the fortune that he had worked so hard to accumulate.

Approximately a decade later, Stone's former residence was converted into an upscale nightclub. The nightclub was later succeeded by a number of restaurants that have included the Lamplighter, the Forte, Copperfields, P.J. Ruggles, Robinson's and Savannah's. Today, this century-old building serves as home to the Spring Lake Manor, a restaurant and banquet facility.

The Pazienzas

The Pazienza family emigrated from the mountainous region of northern Italy to the United States in the early 1900s. They settled in the Villa Park area, where the original family members resided on the 600 block of Prospect Avenue for many years.

In Italy, the Pazienzas had been revered for their adeptness at cutting fine stone from mountains, which was used to build walls, walkways and steps. Locally, in the early part of the twentieth century, the Pazienza name was associated with the installation of several bluestone sidewalks along certain streets in Sea Girt and Spring Lake.

In addition to stone cutting, the Pazienzas were also very successful at land cultivation. Their creative talents and appreciation of the soil led a few members of the family to develop into full landscape gardeners. For several decades, Michael Pazienza Sr. owned and operated a popular nursery and garden center on a tract of land that bordered State Highway 71 between Ocean Road and Prospect Avenue. There, he enjoyed raising and selling small trees and shrubs.

In the early 1960s, Pazienza sold his property to Central Jersey Bank and purchased a florist's shop owned by Bill Herbert at the corner of the highway and Snyder Avenue. Herbert's Florist was extensive and included the corner property on the southwest side of Wall Road to where the Hill and Dale Nursery School is presently located.

For nearly ten years, Pazienza and his son, Mike Jr., operated a florist's shop that enjoyed a loyal and steady following. However, the business abruptly came to an end in 1971, when the senior Pazienza suffered a paralyzing stroke. Ocean First Bank currently occupies the florist's former site. Mike Pazienza Jr. has maintained a local landscaping business and proudly carries forth with a beloved family tradition.

A Word about the Pound Fisherman

In the 1900s, the lucrative pound fishing industry was more than an occupation at the Jersey Shore; it was a way of life. The season lasted from March through December, with the peak taking place between May and October. During the winter months, the fishing crews worked in shacks along the beaches, assembling the nets needed for the new fishing season.

The fish, usually an assortment of shad, mackerel and herring, were caught in nets that were attached to a series of ropes and poles located a short distance from the shoreline. Each day, an open boat was lugged over the beach to the shoreline on wooden rollers, pulled by horses that were usually Clydesdales. When the boat approached the surf, the fishing crew would unhook the horses and leap into the boat, rowing to the pound site. The nets were then pulled to the side of the boat, where crew members used either small hand nets or large woven baskets to scoop out the fish. After the catch, the large nets were dropped back into the water for another twenty-four-hour period. Ultimately, the fish were cleaned and readied for market.

Pound fishing was enormously hard work, and it was performed in almost all types of weather. In the early 1900s, many pound fisheries existed along the coast of both Monmouth and Ocean Counties, with two of the fisheries located in Spring Lake. Several of these fishing crews, including pound owners like Joseph Brown, lived in and around the Lake Como and Villa Park areas.

8

THE 1920s

A Borough Is Formed

According to some area historians, the 1920s roared at the shore. From rumrunners to speakeasies, few coastal regions were left untouched by Prohibition.

While Lake Como and Villa Park remained mostly on the fringe of the Jazz Age's illicit activities, local lore has suggested a few notable exceptions. Two speakeasies were conducted at separate locations on Highway 4N in the north end of town, while on Ocean Road, a residential garage supposedly served as headquarters for a bootlegging operation in 1925.

Aside from these particular sites, though, historically speaking, the majority of residents of Lake Como and Villa Park had very little or nothing to do with Prohibition and were much more concerned about how to deal with existing conditions in their neighborhoods. Before the end of the decade, these residents' overwhelming concerns would finally be addressed.

A Time of Discontent

The areas that had come to be known as Lake Como and Villa Park were a part of Wall Township's Fourth District. As these two areas grew more populous during the 1920s, their residents became increasingly unhappy with the township's neglect of the district. Poor roads and the lack of gas, electric and telephone service to many of the streets and neighborhoods were reasons enough to bring together residents for a meeting in the autumn of 1926.

This group of residents, led by Martha Brown Wickham, convened at a garage behind Brown's Gas Station in Lake Como, where they discussed the need for improvements in the district. At Martha Wickham's urging, the group adopted a name for their organization and elected officers. William Senkel, a local merchant, was elected president of the newly formed Fourth District Improvement Association.

The following week, a second meeting was held, at which time several members of the association broached the subject of whether or not the district should secede from Wall Township. When the subject of secession was discussed with individuals outside the meeting place, not everyone in Lake Como and Villa Park was in favor of such a move. For some, the move seemed too radical. Tensions began to build between those who approved of forming a new borough and those who wished to remain part of Wall Township.

In November 1926, the association held a barn dance at Brown's garage in an attempt to promote goodwill and bridge the differences between the two sides. The dance was also used as a means to raise funds for the legal expenses the group expected to incur in the coming months. Before the year was concluded, the association had formed a committee to explore possible names for a new borough.

The association's next meeting, held in January 1927, was moved to the Spring Lake Community House due to the need for a larger meeting space. Although the association held an election for new officers, only one of the organization's original officers was replaced. William Senkel remained its president, and Charles Vanderhoef was selected to serve as the group's sergeant-at-arms.

By spring, events were occurring in rapid order as the organization completed the necessary legal steps to become officially known as the Spring Lake Heights Improvement Association. In April, association members succeeded in having a bill for incorporation

A westward glance toward the corner of Wall Road and the state highway in 1921. *Courtesy of John Miller.*

pushed through the state legislature as they continued to campaign openly for change. While opponents of the bill had vocalized their objections to it, none had undertaken any significant measures to prevent the bill's passage in the legislature.

Residents who felt they could defeat the secession issue at a later date were suddenly surprised when Governor A. Harry Moore signed the bill, thereby authorizing residents of the Fourth District to hold a special election regarding secession. The election was promptly scheduled for May 3, 1927, in the lobby of the Newark Guest House in Villa Park.

In the preceding months, there had been several incidents of name-calling and even a few harsh verbal exchanges between members of the two sides. However, on election day, voters were quiet and orderly, in spite of the fact that fourteen votes had to be discounted for various reasons. Out of the 518 ballots that qualified, 280 votes were in favor of secession and 238 votes were against it. Spring Lake Heights had become the last municipality to be formed out of an original section of Wall Township.

Election and Administrative Appointments

The borough's first official election took place on May 31, 1927, at which time residents elected a mayor, six council members, a collector and a town assessor. A friendly rivalry developed between the residents of the north and the south ends of town as they stumped for the candidates who were from their particular sections.

When all the votes were tabulated, Roderick Allgor had been elected to serve as the first mayor of Spring Lake Heights. Allgor defeated Captain Herbert L. Davis, a World War I veteran, for the mayoral post. Allgor had a rich ancestral heritage, as he was a direct descendant of Lord Neil Campbell, an officer in the Revolutionary War who later served as one of New Jersey's early governors. The Allgor family's presence in Monmouth County dated back to the 1700s.

The borough's newly elected councilmen were Samuel Jeffries, Harry Larsen, Walter Pearce, Herman Bennett, Andrew Pearce and Allan Wickham. Wickham was later appointed to the position of council president by Mayor Allgor. Each council member was either a local craftsman or a retail operator. William Senkel was elected to serve as the town's first assessor, while Adelaide Craig won the post of borough collector.

Spring Lake Heights held its first organizational meeting at the Como Grammar School nearly a week later, on June 6. During the meeting, the mayor made appointments to several key committees, which included finance, fire, police, streets, lights, sanitation and water. Ellsworth Lutz was appointed the police chief and constable. Marie Adele Pierce was named borough treasurer, while J. Edgar Brown was asked to serve as the borough clerk until the following January. In his newly appointed position, Brown was granted permission to buy a borough seal and an ordinance and minute book, plus other stationery.

Council meetings were set for the second and fourth Mondays of the month at 8:00 p.m. in the Lake Como Grammar School.

Independent Fire Company No. 1, Spring Lake Heights

Once Spring Lake Heights had officially attained its borough status, many of its residents rolled up their sleeves and looked for ways to volunteer and improve the town. It was this sense of community spirit that led thirteen male residents to meet in April 1928 at S.D. Hurley's Cement Block Plant on Monmouth Avenue. The purpose of this meeting was to explore ways to organize and finance a fire department in their new borough. Up to this point, fire protection for Lake Como and Villa Park had been provided by the Spring Lake Fire Company. This group of men agreed to continue meeting at the plant until they were able to find land for the construction of a firehouse.

The group's second meeting proved even more productive, as they held an election for executive officers, formed committees and informally named themselves the Independent Fire Company of Spring Lake Heights. This name was later changed to Independent Fire Company No. 1, Spring Lake Heights, as it appeared on the company's official charter of incorporation.

Little remained in the wake of a devastating fire at the Ahern Lumber Yard on Monmouth Avenue and the railroad in September 1971. *Courtesy of the Veltre family.*

After eight months of hard work, the firemen were able to build a firehouse on two lots that had been owned by Timothy Hurley between Essex and Sussex Avenues. All of the construction work was done by the company members, with many of the members donating furniture and electrical fixtures for the project. Lumber was generously given by three local lumber companies. Funding for the project came from a variety of sources, including cash donations, cake sales, raffles and festivals. A carnival fundraiser was held on the northwest corner of Warren Avenue and the highway in the summer of 1928.

The first meeting of the Independent Fire Company No. 1, Spring Lake Heights, took place in the company's new building on December 14, 1928. Four months later, an election for the first line officers was held, whereby William Jackson was elected as the company's first fire chief. The company's first fire truck was purchased in May 1929.

Over the course of time, the organization benefited greatly from the continuous fundraising efforts of its Ladies' Auxiliary. On several occasions, the auxiliary's donations helped with the company's purchase of new trucks and the construction of an additional bay in the firehouse.

In 1960, ground was broken for the construction of a new three-bay firehouse at Sixth and Essex Avenues. The site was located just south of the original building. An addition to the new building followed in the early 1970s.

Throughout its eighty-year history, the fire company has responded to many house fires, along with some extraordinary blazes in the borough. These blazes have included the original Wall Methodist Church, the Beau Rivage Restaurant, Ahern's Lumberyard, the Old Mill Inn, Georgio's Restaurant and the Spring Lake Golf Club. The current members of this organization continue to give unselfishly of their time and service to the community.

9
THE ENSUING YEARS

The Town Center

For several years following the borough's incorporation, many residents continued to refer to the two former sections of town by their earlier names: Villa Park and Lake Como. The borough's total population during the 1930s was about eight hundred residents, and that number slowly increased over the next two decades.

The center of Spring Lake Heights was on a triangular-shaped piece of property at the junction of Allaire Road and the highway. A professional building currently occupies the site. During the 1930s and '40s, this property served as home for McClains meat market, a grocery store, an icehouse, a gas station and Tony's Barber Shop.

The grocery store had existed prior to the 1920s and had been operated by Weston Rice. The store was later renovated and acquired by Drummond "Drum" Thorn in 1937. The Vanderhoefs, one of the earliest families in Lake Como, operated a similar store across the highway from Thorn's.

For many years, the town's post office had been managed in Rice's store. However, by the late 1930s, the post office was moved to Vanderhoef's, where Mrs. Vanderhoef served as postmistress.

Left: By 1937, Drummond "Drum" Thorn had purchased and remodeled Rice's former store. *Courtesy of Jean Worthington.*

Below: Prior to the 1920s and throughout the following decade, Weston Rice operated a popular grocery store at the junction of the highway and Church Street. *Courtesy of Jean Worthington.*

She was succeeded in her position by Mrs. Morton in 1948. Eventually, these types of post offices ceased operating when regular home mail delivery was put into effect by the United States Postal Service.

The Great Depression

The Great Depression of the 1930s brought severe economic hardship to vast numbers of residents throughout the shore. Many of the area's homes were occupied by "extended families," a situation whereby several generations of one family resided together due to financial constraints. Throughout the decade, there were sad reminders of individuals who had fallen into the era's darkest depths. One resident of the borough still recalled how his family prepared a fried egg sandwich and a cup of coffee for a man who had knocked on the family's front door looking for a meal. Locally, several small grocers and a coal yard provided food and fuel to needy residents free of charge.

Since much of Spring Lake Heights consisted of farmland, many homeowners cultivated vegetable gardens to help supplement their dietary needs. This practice continued throughout World War II, when food rationing became a regular and necessary part

Members of the Bennett family at their chicken farm near Wall Road. *Courtesy of the Wickham family.*

Above: Susan Ludlow Wickham and son Claude assist a young neighbor on one of their horses in 1924. *Courtesy of the Wickham family.*

Opposite, top: Elva and Warren Huellit at their family's farm on Wall Road around 1915. *Courtesy of the Veltre family.*

Opposite, bottom: Anna Mae Craig plays with the family's dog at their property near the highway in 1929. *Courtesy of the Wickham family.*

of American life due to wartime conservation. "It was neighbor helping neighbor," remembered one resident who grew up in the Villa Park area. A pig farmer who lived at the present corner of Fox Hollow Drive and Old Mill Road often shared his pigs with neighbors on Ocean Road and Warren Avenue. Chickens were raised by homeowners throughout the town.

Most residents relied on the simple pleasures of life to help them through the period's adversities. Reading, card playing and front porch conversations offered respites from daily tensions. Many of the borough's children fished at the Old Mill Pond, while others hunted for golf balls around the foundation of a former icehouse. The icehouse, which had suffered a fire at the end of the 1920s, had once stood across from the current site of the borough's waterworks building. A swimming hole, located behind Pond Road, was used by dozens of children throughout the summer months.

The Airport

During a part of the 1930s, an airport operated in the north end of town. The airport contained two runways, one that ran parallel to Allaire Road, ending at Old Mill Road, and another that ran from Allaire Road to Wall Road. A huge wooden hanger, which housed up to four planes, was located near the western boundary of the Brown-Wickham farm, currently Wyckham Manor.

For approximately five years, the airport served as home to the Deluxe Flying Service, where interested parties could pay a three-dollar fee to ride the skies over the Spring Lake Heights area. Each plane was capable of transporting six to eight people at a time. The airport could have been considered somewhat of an anomaly, having operated during the years of the Great Depression. However, the business enjoyed great popularity among curiosity-seekers and wealthy vacationers who stayed at the hotels in nearby Spring Lake.

The Deluxe Flying Service was later grounded when one of its pilots crashed into a tree on the north side of Wall Road, killing two people. In a lesser-known incident, another pilot created panic when he deliberately "swooped" an estate on Ocean Avenue in Spring Lake after having argued with the estate's owner. The incident not only terrorized the estate's residents but many of the nearby beachgoers as well.

After the airport's closing, the immense property served as a ball field, a polo field and an informal golf driving range. In 1951, the property was purchased by the Homestead Development Company for the construction of homes.

Frank Gaskin's Dairy

Throughout much of this era and up until 1950, Frank Gaskin and his family operated a dairy located behind a house on Warren Avenue near the railroad crossing and the current site of TD Bank. Many town and area residents patronized this dairy, whose business slogan was almost as popular as the products themselves: "You can whip our cream, but you can't beat our milk."

Les Gordon's Truck Company

Les Gordon's company was located on the north side of Ocean Road in an area between the Villa Park Chapel and the Villa Park School. Drivers for the company were dispatched to seafood plants in southern New Jersey, where they loaded their trucks with clams and shellfish. After leaving the plant, the drivers transported the seafood to Fulton's Fish Market in New York City. A private home now occupies the truck company's former site.

The Tip Top Bread Company

During the 1940s, the Tip Top Bread Company operated a small distribution center in a barn located behind Brown's Garage, at the corner of Ludlow Avenue and the highway. Bread orders were transported by a tractor-trailer from the company's manufacturing plant in northern New Jersey. Upon reaching Spring Lake Heights, the bread was unloaded onto six waiting trucks, and local deliverymen distributed the orders to various stores and restaurants throughout the county.

The Spring Lake Heights Elementary School

The Spring Lake Heights Elementary School was built in 1938 on land donated to the borough by Roderick Allgor, the town's first mayor. In addition to providing a kindergarten-through-eighth-grade education to its students, the school also provided a common link between the two former sections of the borough.

Although the school's overall enrollment increased in the following decades, the class sizes remained relatively small for the first couple years. When borough resident Ralph Newman graduated in 1941, he was one of only thirteen students in the eighth-grade class.

Compared to the educational institutions of today, the new Spring Lake Heights Elementary School had far fewer amenities. However, students who attended the school throughout the 1940s and '50s hold only fond memories of their alma mater. One alumnus described the school's atmosphere as having been similar to that of a big family.

He especially remembered the day in 1953 when a black-and-white television set was brought into a classroom in order for the students to watch the inauguration of President Eisenhower.

The school's small but very active PTO provided the pupils with cupcake parties, holiday treats and lively skits and shows in which the PTO members themselves performed. In the place of a library, books were brought into the classrooms on rolling shelves. A community nurse from the Health Center in Manasquan was dispatched to the school when needed.

Renowned local artist Mabel Burr visited the school several times a week to teach art to the students. Since there was no formal music

A pen-and-ink sketch of the former Como Railroad Station by renowned local artist Mabel Burr. Mrs. Burr taught art to borough students at the Spring Lake Heights Elementary School during the 1950s. *Courtesy of the Wickham family.*

Left: Students pose by the school Christmas tree in the building's main hall, 1940. *Courtesy of the Veltre family.*

Below: The Spring Lake Heights Elementary School's first-grade class performs *Hiawatha* at the Spring Lake Community House in 1946. *Courtesy of the Veltre family.*

The eighth-grade graduation class of 1953. *Courtesy of the Veltre family.*

room or auditorium at the school, Mrs. Braley, a music teacher and Brighton Avenue resident, provided music instruction to each of the classes. After school, she gave voice and piano lessons to several students at her home.

All school shows were performed at the Spring Lake Community House, while the eighth-grade graduation was held at the Como Methodist Church on Church Street. Janice Veltre and Betty Hosner fondly recalled their school graduation and how they joined with other classmates in decorating the church with bunches of laurel collected from yards on Wall Road. Following their commencement, the class of 1953 attended a special graduation dinner at the Beau Rivage Restaurant, which was formerly located at the southwest corner of Warren Avenue and Old Mill Road. Mrs. Veltre's husband, Frank, later served as the school's beloved custodian.

By the late 1950s, a new gymnasium had been added to the school. The welcomed addition enabled the school to hold student dances and, at long last, to have a basketball team.

Ground was broken in the early 1970s for a new addition that included more classroom space, a multipurpose room, a kitchen and a library. As the town's population increased, the school once again undertook an expansion and renovation program in 2002.

The school continues to provide borough students with one of the finest and most progressive education programs at the Jersey Shore.

The Old Mill

Nestled in the southwest corner of the borough is one of the Jersey Shore's most popular restaurants, the Mill at Spring Lake Heights. Today, the restaurant is frequented by many for dinners, receptions and charity galas. However, in 1720, this picturesque spot beside the pond and stream served as the site for southern Monmouth County's earliest gristmill. In addition to grinding grains for the area's farmers, it is believed that a portion of the building was also used for tanning leathers. Local historians are uncertain why the

The Old Mill Inn, pictured here in the 1960s. The former gristmill was converted into a popular restaurant in 1938. *Courtesy of the Veltre family.*

gristmill was eventually torn down and have cited the region's sparse population as a possible reason.

By the early 1800s, though, Howell Township had been established, and more farmers had settled into the southern parts of the county. In 1823, two brothers, John and Charles King of Essex, England, moved to Monmouth County and purchased a substantial tract of land located next to a stream. The brothers paid $1,000 for ninety-three acres of property that are now considered part of Spring Lake Heights.

Following this purchase, they proceeded to build a gristmill at the location. As was the case a century earlier, the new mill also carried the distinction of being the only one of its kind in southern Monmouth County. For the next twenty-eight years, local farmers, who had previously trekked to other parts of the region with their grains, now enjoyed the convenience of having a gristmill located closer to home.

In 1851, the Osbourne family assumed ownership of the mill and operated the business for nearly forty years before it suffered a devastating fire.

In approximately 1890, Zebulon "Zeb" Stillwell, a local resident, erected a new gristmill at the same site. George and Thomas Franklin operated the business for Stillwell, whose mill not only prospered but also enjoyed the reputation of being one of the cleanest and most organized in the county.

However, by the end of the 1920s, Stillwell's mill had suffered a sharp decline in business, as more farm owners were relying largely on "grinders" to pulverize their grains. Less than a decade later, most farmers had dispensed with the use of grinders and directly purchased the grains they needed from food dealers.

When Stillwell finally closed his gristmill in 1937, residents and borough officials speculated on the future of the vacant site. The former mill didn't remain unoccupied for long, however, as restaurateur William Brauweiler purchased and converted the building into a restaurant the following year. Brauweiler named his new venture the Old Mill.

For diners, the restaurant's lakeside setting was one of its most engaging features. Inside, patrons enjoyed a cozy ambiance that reflected a mostly early American décor. The restaurant's popular taproom, its walls mounted with various game heads, had once served as the main part of Stillwell's gristmill.

By the early 1990s, the inn was also featuring weekend dinner shows in addition to its elegant cuisine. Many of the shows included luminaries from the stage and screen.

In its seventy-four-year history, the restaurant suffered through three significant fires, all of which were electrical in origin. In February 1969, a fire extensively damaged the building's first floor and bar area. Eleven years later, the restaurant's first floor and parts of its exterior sustained damage from a fire caused by a short circuit in wires that led to an outside patio bar. In both cases, the inn remained closed for several weeks while repairs were made.

The third fire, in August 1985, proved to be the most catastrophic, as it completely destroyed the beloved landmark. The Spring Lake Heights fire company was joined by three neighboring fire departments in trying to extinguish the blaze, which at one point was so intense that no one was able to get within twenty-five feet of the building.

The situation worsened when a natural gas line, located underneath the restaurant, erupted and continued to fuel the fire. By the time gas company officials were able to shut down the line, the historic inn was a raging inferno. When the fire was finally brought under control at sunrise, very little of the inn remained.

Ultimately, the devastating fire marked the end of only a chapter in the restaurant's history. A new dining facility was built at the site and reopened for business in 1987. Two millstones, which were incorporated into the new building's décor, were the only artifacts that remained from the former gristmill. The restaurant has continued as one of the shore's top choices for dining.

History on the Corner

The century-old building at 569 Church Street is currently home to Hoffman's, one of the best-recognized names in homemade ice cream on the Jersey Shore. In earlier years, this corner site was

The Lily Ann Tearoom as it appeared in 1960 at the corner of Church Street and Highway 71. The popular eatery operated for more than two decades. *Courtesy of Jean Worthington.*

occupied by a couple notable businesses, among them the renowned Lily Ann Tearoom.

Nearly thirty years before opening their locally celebrated tearoom, Spring Lake residents William and Marguerite Morris operated a grocery store in a building they owned at the junction of Church Street and the state highway in Lake Como. The couple maintained the business throughout World War I before they relinquished their space to another grocer in 1920.

The new store was short-lived, however, as an extensive fire swept through the building in 1922 and rendered the place uninhabitable. Sam Jeffries, a local contractor, was put in charge of the clean-up work, which took well over a year to complete. Jeffries salvaged what he could of the original structure before he went to work at remodeling. He altered a few of the building's former features and added larger picture windows near the front entrance. These windows gave the edifice the more open appearance it has today.

The renovation was completed by the latter part of the decade and the building then stood ready for occupation. Within a short amount of time, the Holland Bulb Company, a flower mail-order business, was opened at the site. The flower company, which was somewhat unique for the shore area, was operated by two brothers, both of whom were from the Netherlands. While one brother remained at the retail operation on Church Street, the other sibling spent the majority of his days in Holland processing and shipping the company's orders.

After a few years, postal authorities launched a full investigation of the brothers and their activities due to the large number of complaints they had received from the company's clients, all of whom had paid for orders they had not received. Ultimately, the investigation revealed the brothers' intentional misuse of funds. The brother from the retail outlet was arrested and deported by government officials. Both Dutchmen were barred from ever returning to the United States.

Following the departure of the flower company, a luncheonette briefly occupied the space before the Morrises decided to embark on a new venture at their site. In the preceding years, Marguerite Morris had been managing a restaurant in Ocean Grove and was quite anxious to own a similar business. Frequently, she and her family had eaten at a popular tearoom in the Asbury Park area. After numerous visits there, Mrs. Morris was thoroughly convinced that a similar type of eatery could be a great success in Spring Lake Heights.

After some meticulous planning, the Morrises opened the Lily Ann Tearoom in 1943. The restaurant was named for the couple's daughters, Lily and Ann.

For more than twenty-five years, the tearoom presented some of the finest meals served anywhere along the Jersey Shore. The restaurant's chief chef, Werner Duck, guided the kitchen staff in preparing many savory menu items, including sweet relish and buttermilk biscuits, two of the eatery's signature side dishes.

The combination of Duck's culinary skills and the Morrises' insistence on the use of fresh ingredients produced winning reviews for the tearoom. When Mrs. Morris discovered the "back-up" chef preparing croquettes with the less-desirable parts of a chicken, she firmly reminded him that only the best parts were to be used at all times. William Morris shopped for fresh produce at local farm markets each morning.

Sizzling T-bone steaks, served on iron platters, were one of the restaurant's most requested entrees. Roast turkey and pork with sauerkraut were equally as popular. Before the arrival of the meal, each diner was given a small scoop of orange sherbet to cleanse their palates.

Most of the tearoom's clientele were local residents and vacationers from New York and Philadelphia. Jim and Don Ameche, popular actors of the 1940s and '50s, often dined there, as did the various performers from the Ivy Tower Playhouse in Spring Lake. The mother of legendary stage and screen actor Gordon MacRae dined at the tearoom nearly every night. Frequently, she lingered over her meal while writing letters to her son.

The restaurant's seating capacity was 124 patrons. During the busy summer months, it was not uncommon to have had the same number of people outside the building waiting to be seated. The business was open from May through October, and the Morris family labored there six days a week. No matter how fatigued she may have been, Mrs. Morris always took the time to speak with every person who passed through the eatery's front door. In addition to the outstanding home-cooked meals, it was Marguerite Morris's sincere interest in her patrons that endeared so many of them to the tearoom.

The restaurant's highly successful run came to a close when the couple decided to retire in 1965. The family maintained ownership of the building until William Morris's death a decade later. The tearoom was succeeded by a couple similar restaurants before Hoffman's Ice Cream opened at the location in 1986.

10

GOLFING IN SPRING LAKE HEIGHTS

During the late 1890s, the game of golf had just been introduced in America, and its popularity spread quickly throughout the country, especially in the eastern half of the United States. In 1909, the Spring Lake Real Estate Company purchased a 118-acre farm alongside what is now known as Warren Avenue in Spring Lake Heights. The farm, which had previously belonged to James Thompson, a sea captain from Manasquan, had been in Thompson's family since the 1860s. This extensive property was developed into a lush and scenic golf course, which is presently the privately owned Spring Lake Golf Club.

As interest continued to spike in the game, some local residents even went so far as to use portions of their properties for practice areas and makeshift putting greens.

Aside from the newly organized Spring Lake Golf Course, there were no other formal golfing facilities in or around Lake Como or Villa Park. However, with the help of a few golf enthusiasts, the situation would soon change.

3

REPLACE DIVOTS

4

SPRING LAKE GOLF & COUNTRY CLUB

HOLES	YARDS	PAR	STROKES	1	2	3	4	WON X LOST
10	150	3	17					
11	315	4	12					
12	530	5	2					
13	445	4	5					
14	325	4	13					
15	355	4	10					
16	255	4	15					
17	410	4	6					
18	390	4	8					
	3175	36	IN					

OUT

TOTAL

The Homestead Golf Club

Until 1920, much of the land around Allaire Road was woods, fields or farmlands. One of the largest farms was owned by Ezekial Allen, whose property included the area that is currently occupied by Fairway Mews Townhouses and Golf Club. During the 1880s, Allen sold his farm to Pitney Curtis, a local sea captain who had formerly owned the Manasquan "Squan" Turnpike. For nearly four decades, the Curtis farm raised turkeys, pigs and assorted produce that was either sold to nearby hotels and tearooms or used in bartering arrangements with other farmers locally.

In 1921, the Curtis farmhouse, a large three-story home, was transformed into the Homestead Golf Club by a group of local businessmen, all of whom were golf aficionados. They engaged the services of Robert Trent Jones, the renowned master planner of golf courses, to design the layout of the newly acquired property.

The property conversion was met with both curiosity and enthusiasm by area residents and vacationers. Ultimately, the new course drew an appreciable number of golfers in spite of the fact that some of the fairways contained dry and rough patches due to inadequate irrigation.

Far left: A scorecard from the Spring Lake Golf and Country Club, circa 1930s. *Courtesy of the Wickham family.*

Middle: Three golfers navigate the fairway at the Homestead Golf Course during the late 1920s. *Courtesy of the Wickham family.*

Left: The Homestead Golf Course contained numerous rough patches before it was renovated in the mid-1940s. *Courtesy Wickham Family*

By the mid-1940s, the club had been purchased by Tony Yonadi, a savvy entrepreneur who immediately went to work and upgraded the property considerably. Yonadi expanded the size of the greens and planted numerous trees along much of the eighteen-hole course. An irrigation system was installed to provide water to the fairways on a regular basis. The clubhouse was extensively renovated to include a new pro shop, a cocktail lounge and an upscale restaurant, which became well known for its outstanding cuisine.

By the end of the decade, the Homestead Golf and Country Club had evolved into one of New Jersey's most popular semi-private courses. The club hosted golfers from as far away as Philadelphia, Long Island and Westchester, New York. During special tournaments, the participating players represented an even broader geographic range.

Golfers played at the course year-round, weather permitting. While membership dues were $300 per year, non-members were welcome to play at any time for a much smaller fee.

In the early 1950s, Roddy Newman was hired to serve as the club's golf pro. Throughout his tenure, Newman taught a steady stream of students, all of whom were anxious to either learn or improve their golf games. Lessons at the club took place daily between 8:00 a.m. and 12:00 p.m., and students paid four dollars each for the half hour of instruction. The junior lessons for young boys and girls were especially popular.

Each season, the club employed local teenagers to serve as caddies for the golfers. One former resident of the borough fondly recalled being hired to retrieve balls during Newman's golf lessons. Often, he found himself climbing under bushes or venturing into out-of-the-way places such as streams to fetch the stray balls. Looking for golf balls became a favorite hobby among the local teenagers, many of whom willingly risked a reprimand by the club's officials for entering the premises without permission.

While the Homestead's management frowned on most intrusions, it more than welcomed all area residents to the club's giant fireworks display held each July 4. The holiday celebration, which was free of charge, was attended by scores of spectators who viewed the event from a designated lawn near the main golf course. Most of the attendees sat comfortably on either blankets or beach towels they had brought from home.

Throughout the years, there were dozens of glittering affairs held at the club. One of the most notable was the annual Essex County Democratic Golf Outing, at which time a huge tent was placed on the grounds for a lavish dinner and cocktail party. The political fundraiser often attracted several hundred golfers, while the cocktail party and dinner was attended by more than one thousand guests.

Former president John F. Kennedy appeared at the event in 1959 and again in 1960 while he was still serving as a Massachusetts senator and campaigning for his party's nomination for president. Kennedy was met by very enthusiastic supporters on both occasions, many of whom sought a handshake or some sort of personal acknowledgment from the young presidential hopeful.

Former New Jersey governor Robert Meyner also attended the event for several consecutive years. Club officials accommodated Governor Meyner's preference for tennis by installing a special tennis court near one of the fairways.

This postcard depicts a scene from the early days of the Homestead Golf Course. *Courtesy of John Miller.*

Indeed, this was a prestigious era for the golf club and its restaurant, which was considered one of the shore's most chic gathering spots. The restaurant provided a choice dining venue, not only for the politically famous, but also for a variety of vacationing celebrities and prominent business leaders.

Motorists who passed by the Homestead's impressive circular entrance on Allaire Road often took note of the elegantly attired doorman and the various guests who were being assisted into the club.

By the 1970s, however, the club's illustrious run had come to a close as developers sought to purchase the property. Their plans called for the construction of Fairway Mews Golf and Racquet Club, a 560-unit luxury town house development that would provide for a 4,010-yard par-sixty executive golf course. The proposal also included plans for a swimming pool, tennis courts, a pro shop and a clubhouse.

Initially, the Homestead's conversion was met with both shock and mixed emotions by local residents, and the project was actually delayed several times due to changes in the property's ownership. However, by the latter part of the decade, construction at the site had resumed, and the first section of Fairway Mews was selling out before the units were even completed. For area residents who had raised their families and were living alone, Fairway Mews offered an attractive alternative to remaining in a large home. Career couples and individuals also found the town houses both desirable and convenient.

Ron Chamura, a PGA professional, was named director of golf and tennis at the club.

The Homestead Restaurant, which operated independently of Fairway Mews, continued to be a popular spot for dining and catering. Following the Yonadi family's tenure, the restaurant experienced several changes in management and ownership. By 1992, the banquet facility had been renamed the Spring Lake Heights Manor, and the restaurant's name was changed to Georgio's.

During the early morning hours of September 18, 1992, an enormous fire broke out in the restaurant. The blaze began near the front hallway and spread very quickly to other parts of the building. More than one hundred firefighters from three neighboring communities joined Spring Lake Heights firemen in trying to contain the inferno, which burned out of control for several hours. Fairway Mews residents waited anxiously throughout the night as firefighters worked relentlessly to prevent the blaze from spreading to the neighboring complexes. The fire produced an endless stream of sparks and ashes that were carried by a light and steady breeze to points east of Highway 71.

By the following day, the celebrated restaurant had been reduced to a blackened shell. Amidst the ruins, only a long canopied awning at the former front entrance remained intact, providing both local residents and former guests with a poignant link to the Homestead Golf and Country Club's storied past.

II

THE POSTWAR PERIOD AND BEYOND

The 1950s

After the long and difficult years of the Great Depression followed by the country's entry into World War II, the 1950s ushered in an era of unbridled optimism and prosperity for the nation. Under the administration of President Dwight D. Eisenhower, the country's economy soared to a level not seen in more than two decades.

The economic boom was felt in varying degrees along the Jersey Shore, where previously undeveloped properties were suddenly transformed into vacation playgrounds that included new homes, summer cottages, motels and retail establishments.

The new Garden State Parkway enabled scores of travelers to reach coastal destinations in a more efficient manner. Prior to its construction, motorists spent a longer time navigating the limited number of roads that led from the northern parts of the state to the various shore towns.

As tourism increased, families from outside southern Monmouth County became more acquainted with the region and gradually acquired summer homes here or relocated to the shore permanently. While many sought locations close to the coastline, populations slowly increased in the more inland areas as well.

By the early 1950s, the Homestead Development Company had broken ground for the construction of single-family homes on Allaire Road. Additionally, there were a few smaller development sites at properties in the south end of town, near Park Avenue, Ocean Road and Prospect Avenue. By the middle of the decade, ten new homes had been completed on tracts of land located between Wall Road and Allaire Road. Each of these homes sold for $9,900.

However, despite these pockets of construction, Spring Lake Heights, overall, remained a quiet community, and its growth moved at a slower rate than other shore towns at the time. Numerous wooded areas and several unfinished roads lent a rustic feeling to some sections of the borough, and a few sites drew close comparisons to what was usually viewed deep in the countryside. Chicken coops and even turkey houses still existed at some properties.

In addition to grape arbors and walnut groves, a few of the original farms also contained small apple or pear orchards. During the peak of the spring and summer seasons, there were whole masses of bridal wreath, laurel and lilac bushes in yards and fields throughout the town, and blackberries grew wild in many spots. A large chicken farm stood at the eastern edge of Keith Avenue, while corn was grown regularly on land located west of Greve Avenue. Keith and Greve Avenues had rough and unpaved surfaces, and both streets had to be graded by a road crew every couple months.

Local gypsy sightings had diminished by the 1950s. Prior to the start of the decade, it was not unusual for bands of gypsies to have been seen roaming through town either on foot or in vehicles, looking for chickens, garden vegetables or just about any object that could be accessed easily from a property. Most borough residents took the situation pretty much in stride, though, and in some cases even offered light food and water to gypsies who had knocked on their doors looking for a donation.

Vehicular traffic was fairly minimal, even on roads such as State Highway 4N, whose name had been changed to Highway 71 by the 1960s. This artery provided the main link between the borough and neighboring communities and was used regularly by residents for their local travel needs.

This route stood in sharp contrast to State Highway 35, located a short distance away in Wall Township. Highway 35, bordered mostly by woods and fields, had little retail development on it and handled a mere fraction of the traffic seen there today. The road was so infrequently used that most borough residents referred to it as "the back highway."

During this time, Wall Road was of narrower width and less traveled on, to the point where children used the course for sleigh riding after significant snowfalls. A small grocery store and luncheonette stood at the western end of Wall Road throughout much of the decade. Prior to this period, a women's clothing factory had operated for a short interval near the southeast corner of Wall and Old Mill Roads.

There were several family-owned grocers located within the borough, and all were well patronized by the community. With the exception of an Acme in Belmar and a small A&P in Spring Lake, there were no other major grocery stores in the immediate vicinity. Families and individuals relied on the convenience of the corner grocers for such staples as bread, meats and cans of coffee.

Besides the various farms and an archery range, there were also several sizable estates located along Wall Road. One estate composed an area that is currently occupied by the Shenandoah Apartments complex. On many afternoons, a portion of the estate became a softball field when the property's owner graciously allowed local boys to use her expansive front lawn for softball games.

The neighborhood's youngsters also maintained a keen interest in a nearby farm where a large bull roamed freely. Several of those who had participated in the games recalled their daring at having climbed over the farm's fence to retrieve their lost balls. Although all the former players had managed to find the balls, they barely escaped the charging bull.

For the "less adventurous," an ice cream sundae or a root beer float at Ruth and Phil's was a palatable treat for children and adults alike. The popular sandwich and soda shop, owned by Ruth and Phil Ciallella, was located slightly south of the elementary school. The eatery was patronized by many students who stopped

Bob Worthington operated a grocery store on Highway 71 from 1945 to 1958. A realty office and professional building now occupies the site. *Courtesy of Jean Worthington.*

by after school to enjoy everything from a malted milk to a soft drink and a hamburger.

Farther north on the highway, Mrs. Moore's Bakery was a choice spot for pies, breads and oversized sugar cookies. The bakery's coconut custard pies were the talk of the town.

Those who were raised in the borough during this era have likened their childhood memories to a Norman Rockwell depiction of life in "small-town America." It was a time when nearly all activities centered on home, church and an individual's neighborhood.

Most homes in the borough had a television set by the mid-1950s, and as one former resident remembered, "You watched whatever your father was watching." For a child, the town was filled with simple pleasures that included everything from berry-picking to playing a game of pinball at Jimmy's, a small delicatessen on Route 4N.

An annual Halloween party at the Wall Methodist Church is still counted by many to be among their happiest childhood memories.

Eleanor Miller's Homemade Candies

Eleanor Senkel and Elwood Miller met while they were attending Asbury Park High School in the early 1930s. Although neither of them realized it at the time, their fateful meeting would ultimately lead to marriage and to one of the most creative and successful business ventures in southern Monmouth County.

The high school sweethearts married in 1935 and quickly settled into a bungalow owned by the Senkel family on State Highway 4N in the north end of the borough. As they started a family, the couple decided to relocate to a larger home across the highway.

While Elwood Miller worked as a delivery driver for the Tip Top Bread Company, his wife remained at home to raise the couple's two sons. A progressive thinker by nature, Eleanor started to explore her options for working at home in order to help raise funds for her sons' college education.

Elwood especially thought of his wife's ambition when he came across a homemade candy concession while making a delivery to a luncheonette in Red Bank. He was so impressed by the luncheonette's display of confectionaries that when he later mentioned it to Eleanor, both of them wholeheartedly agreed to further explore the option of candy making.

The Millers immediately contacted the luncheonette's owner, who in turn referred them to Molly Pitcher Candies in Long Branch. There, Eleanor was taught the fine art of making and hand-dipping chocolates.

For the first year, the business was conducted mainly from the Millers' dining room table, where fudge, butter crunch and peanut brittle were the shop's main offerings. The Millers' son John still recalls the many afternoons when he juggled his attention between doing homework and watching customers proceed through the house and into the dining room to make candy purchases.

Gradually, other chocolate treats were added to the selection, and the business outgrew the Millers' dining room. The shop was transferred into the larger living room area, where display cases replaced furniture and the fireplace mantel was consistently adorned

Eleanor Miller's Homemade Candies opened for business in 1954. The shop was operated from the Miller family's home on Route 71. *Courtesy of John Miller.*

with candy molds and seasonal ornaments. All of the candy was packed and stored in the dining room.

The business was operated on a year-round basis, with Easter being the busiest time, followed by the hectic summer tourist season. Business was so brisk at Easter that the Millers had to hire a special police officer to handle the extra highway traffic in front of their home.

By the 1960s, Elwood Miller was dividing his time between a position with the Garden State Parkway and assisting his wife. Their business enjoyed phenomenal success as candy lovers from throughout the shore area flocked to the Millers in search of Easter baskets, chocolate Valentines and other assorted treats.

Above: Elwood Miller often assisted his wife with the business. Here the couple takes an inventory of their stock. *Courtesy of John Miller.*

Left: The Millers worked hard at keeping their display cases full of chocolates and other confections. *Courtesy of John Miller.*

Located on Highway 71 in the north end of the borough, this property formerly belonged to Mayor William Senkel and his family. Senkel's daughter, Eleanor Miller, operated her candy shop here during a portion of the 1980s. *Courtesy of John Miller.*

In 1982, the couple shifted the business from their home to a building on the opposite side of the highway. The new site, which had been previously owned by Eleanor's mother, served as the shop's location for the next five years.

Eleanor's retirement from the business in 1987 marked the end of a long and dedicated thirty-three-year career. Eleanor continued to make fudge for her family and friends, and each year she donated a variety of candies to the annual Christmas Fair at the Wall United Methodist Church.

Today, Eleanor Miller's chocolates are as fondly remembered as the beloved "Candy Lady" herself.

The Next Forty Years

Spring Lake Heights maintained a steady growth throughout the 1960s and '70s as former farms and estates made way for suburban development. This new development came in the form of single-family homes and garden apartment complexes.

Joseph E. Robertson, who served as the town's mayor for most of the decade, was instrumental in the borough's purchase of the Allaire Road park property for $22,000. Mayor Robertson had hoped that the newly acquired park would provide current and future residents with some much-needed recreational facilities.

More than fifty years later, the park's tennis courts, playground, soccer and Little League fields are still enjoyed and fully utilized by the community. A community bulletin board situated at the park's entrance lists the names of those who have been inducted into the Spring Lake Heights Athletic Hall of Fame. All of the past and current residents who are listed here have made outstanding contributions of their time and talents to the borough's recreational

The Allaire Road Park serves the borough's recreational needs. *Courtesy of the author.*

program. Included on the Hall of Fame roster are the names of three of the borough's former mayors: Elwood Malick, Peter Maclearie and Joseph Robertson. In 1997, the Allaire Road Park was dedicated in memory of Joseph Robertson during a town-wide anniversary celebration.

Through the aid of Green Acres funds, the borough later acquired nine additional acres of land near the western end of Ocean Road, where a former estate was transformed into a recreational area. In October 1975, residents joined then-mayor Peter Maclearie as they formally dedicated the new recreational tract known as Bicentennial Park. The park was named to honor the country's 200th anniversary, which was celebrated the following year. Bicentennial Park's tennis courts, ball field and basketball courts continue to provide residents with hours of outdoor pleasure.

The 1960s marked the final years of operation for the Spring Lake Heights Hospital, located at the southeast corner of Wall Road and the highway. For more than two decades, Dr. George Gardiner and his wife, Fanny, a registered nurse, maintained a small medical facility that offered treatment for everything from minor injuries to the more serious illnesses. Certain surgeries were also performed there. Some residents who lived near the hospital often blamed the facility's technical equipment for the difficulties they experienced with their television sets. Despite the complaints, though, most were in agreement that the local treatment center provided them with a more convenient alternative than trekking to the former Fitkin Hospital, now Jersey Shore University Medical Center in Neptune.

By the mid-1970s, a local doctor had purchased the property and transformed the building into a rest home for the elderly. The Spring Lake Heights Rest Home operated for more than twenty-five years before the property was resold and converted into town houses.

As the town's population increased, so did its commercial establishments. Several franchised businesses came to the borough in the 1960s.

One of the area's first 7-Eleven convenience stores opened at the corner of Highway 71 and Ocean Road, only to be followed by the opening of a second franchise located in the north end of town a few years later. A Carvel ice cream store at the corner of the highway and Jersey Avenue enjoyed a steady clientele for nearly two decades.

Throughout town, small independent businesses also prospered, especially during the busy summer season. Doolan's Shore Club, which had begun as a small tavern on the highway in the mid-1950s, expanded to eventually include a large restaurant, banquet facilities, a motor lodge and a swimming pool. The site had served as the original clubhouse for the Spring Lake Golf Club at the beginning of the twentieth century. Another family business, Meehan's Funeral Home, was located on Warren Avenue. The funeral home was well known throughout the shore area.

By the early 1970s, ground had been broken north of Snyder Avenue for the construction of the Heights Shopping Center. At a much earlier period, this land had contained a small pond and a marsh that was filled with cattails and cranberries. During the cold winter months, the pond had been a popular spot for ice-skating. The new shopping complex included an A&P supermarket, plus several smaller stores and a luncheonette. A professional building was later added to the complex. Across from the shopping center, apartments and condominiums eventually replaced the multiple greenhouses that had previously belonged to a Wall Township florist.

In 1971, the Brown-Wickham Homestead, a nineteenth-century landmark that had stood at the corner of the highway and Allaire Road, was purchased by a developer who converted the former farm into Colonial-style town houses. Wyckham Manor now occupies the site.

In the summer of 1977, Spring Lake Heights celebrated the fiftieth anniversary of its incorporation. The milestone was marked by a festive dinner held at the Forte Manor, at which the town's present and past mayors were honored. Then-current mayor Richard Rooney helped in cutting the enormous sheet cake that had been created for the occasion. A parade and town-wide picnic was held later that fall.

As the borough entered into the 1980s, Joseph Robertson was once again serving as mayor and leading a drive for the construction of a new municipal complex. Up until this point, the borough's police headquarters and municipal court had been operating from a converted garage on Mercer Avenue. The building once had been a stable. The municipal offices were crowded into a former farmhouse located on Brighton Avenue near the elementary school. Citing the police department's expansion and the town's increased administrative workload, Mayor Robertson complained that working conditions for borough employees were intolerable.

Many residents agreed with the mayor's assessment, and a referendum was scheduled on the project after petitions with more than one thousand signatures were presented to the council. However, voters initially rejected the referendum and turned down all three questions related to the project. One of the questions had addressed whether the Board of Education should donate land on Brighton Avenue for a new building. Prior to the vote, the board had expressed a willingness to donate the land.

Disappointed but not dissuaded by the negative vote, the persistent mayor and his backers vowed to continue the fight.

Ultimately, voters approved the project, and in 1983, a new municipal building was dedicated at 555 Brighton Avenue. The

The Frank E. Adams Municipal Office Building, 2011. *Courtesy of the author.*

Homes in Spring Lake Heights offer a variety of unique architectural styles. *Courtesy of the author.*

ceremonies opened with a rededication of the town's war memorial, which had been relocated to the new site. The complex would serve as home to the borough's police department, municipal court and all administrative offices.

Less than two years later, residents joined the mayor and borough council members in dedicating the Spring Lake Heights Community Center in memory of their recently departed colleague Cornelius V. Kelly. Mr. Kelly not only had served on the town's council but had also spent much of his time assisting numerous veterans' organizations and seniors' groups in the county.

During the 1980s, the east end of Warren Avenue saw several changes. A large savings bank replaced a long-standing real estate office at the southeast corner of Highway 71 and Warren Avenue. Farther down the street, the former Country Club Motel was converted into The Arbors, an upscale residence for seniors.

By 1981, Susan Murphy's Homemade Ice Cream had been established at the corner of Sixth and Warren Avenues. For nearly twenty-five years, the small specialty shop offered a wide assortment of ice cream products and flavors to its many patrons.

This home reflects the popular Arts and Crafts style. *Courtesy of the author.*

By the mid-1990s, the population of Spring Lake Heights had doubled since the 1960s as vacant properties made way for the construction of additional homes and certain neighborhoods were expanded.

In 1996, the relocation of the Spring Lake Post Office to the Spring Lake Heights Shopping Center brought new energy to the complex, which had lagged in business after the departure of the A&P store nearly a decade earlier. Today, the shopping center bustles with a delicatessen, two restaurants, a dry cleaner, a laundromat and a health food market. It is well patronized by both borough residents and those who live in the surrounding communities.

Freedom Park

On Veteran's Day 2003, officials and residents formally dedicated the Veterans' Monument at Freedom Park, located at the corner of Highway 71 and Allaire Road. This same corner had been the site of a blacksmith shop in 1900. A former student from the town's elementary school is credited with raising the funds needed for the park's construction. While small in size, the park is meticulously maintained and adorned with seasonal plantings. It offers an attractive setting where one can pause and reflect on those in uniform who have served and continue to serve to ensure our country's freedom.

The park also reminds one of the good that is created when a community stands and works together. From its police department and various officials to its beautification committee and school associations, the borough is fortunate to have a great many caring individuals and organizations who labor continuously toward the town's ongoing success.

EPILOGUE

As one glances at the hectic pace of Highway 71, it is difficult to envision a time when elegant stagecoaches traveled regularly on this route, only to be met along the way by farmers in horse-drawn wagons. It is even less easy to imagine an airport having existed in an area now occupied by numerous homes.

As in many of the towns across Monmouth County, Spring Lake Heights has seen tremendous growth and change throughout the decades. However, in today's fast-paced and complex world, the borough has managed to maintain many enduring qualities, including small-town values, natural attributes and key links to the past. Whether it was the business acumen of William Reid or the great faith and kindness demonstrated by Captain Samuel Ludlow, each of the town's forefathers left not only an indelible mark on the landscape but also a rich legacy for future generations to follow.

BIBLIOGRAPHY

Asbury Park Evening Press, May 4, 1927; May 8, 1932; November 23, 1963; February 20, 1965; February 26, 1965.

Asbury Park Journal, March 14, 1885.

Asbury Park Press, August 29, 1975; September 10, 1978.

Brown, Kendy. Article. *Herald*, 1997.

Como Methodist Church. *Historical Sketch and Eighty-fourth Anniversary Program*. April 19, 1953.

Dowd, Gregory E. *The Indians of New Jersey*. Trenton: New Jersey Historical Commission, 1992.

Eckman, Howard. Interview. September 10, 2010.

Ellis, Franklin. *History of Monmouth County, New Jersey*. Philadelphia: P.T. Peck and Co., 1885. Reprint, Shrewsbury, NJ: Shrewsbury Historical Society, 1974.

Gardella, Ann. Interview. October 15, 2008.

Greenwald, Jane. Telephone interview. December 17, 2010.

Hall, Jane. Interview. October 15, 2008.

Harrigan, Barbara K. Telephone interview. March 4, 2011.

Haviland, Leona. Telephone interview. November 30, 2010.

Horner, William S. *This Old Monmouth of Ours*. Freehold, NJ: Moreau Bros., 1932.

Hosner, Betty S. Interview. October 26, 2010.

Jackson, Jeanne. Article. *Asbury Park Press*, September 18, 1992.

Krampert, Marilyn. Interview. March 6, 2011.

Ludlow, Susan. Autograph book. 1878.

Martin, Paul E. "A Bit of History." Research paper, Ocean Lodge, Spring Lake Heights, n.d.

Miller, John. Interview. December 6, 2010.

Newman, Margie and Ralph. Interview. November 5, 2010.

Newman, Ralph. Telephone interview. March 6, 2011.

Old Wall Historical Society. *Wall Township: A Quieter Time*. Wall Township, NJ: LACN Graphics, 1990.

Once Known as Como. N.p., n.d.

Pazienza, Michael. Telephone interview. January 26, 2011.

Policastro, Douglas. Telephone interview. February 6, 2011.

Rice, Gary. Telephone interview. February 5, 2011.

Roper, Grace Trott. *Belmar in Retrospect*. Neptune, NJ: Hoffman Press, 1978.

Salter, Edward. *A History of Monmouth and Ocean Counties*. N.p.: Gardner and Son, 1890.

Shore Holiday News, June 19, 1977; August 19, 1977; October 12, 1977; March 1979; July 1979; July 1980; November 1980; July 2, 1992; August 6, 1992.

Smith, Keith. Interview. February 5, 2011.

Spring Lake: An Early History. Spring Lake, NJ: Bicentennial History Committee, 1976.

Spring Lake Heights Independent Fire Company No. 1. "History of Spring Lake Heights Independent Fire Company No. 1." Seventy-fifth anniversary paper, 2003.

Spring Lake Heights Youth Association Journal, 1948.

Stockton, Frank R. *Stories of New Jersey*. New Brunswick, NJ: Rutgers University Press, 1961.

Talbert, Mrs. Robert. Article. N.p., n.d.

Van Benthuysen, Doug. Article. *Herald*, August 1997.

Veltre, Frank, and Janice Veltre. Interviews. January 30, 2011; February 15, 2011.

Veltre, Janice. Interview. October 26, 2010.

Wall United Methodist Church. *History of Wall United Methodist Church*. Booklet, 1997.

Wickham family. Assorted scrapbooks and memorabilia.

Wickham, Lissa. Articles. *Shore Holiday News*, March 1980; July 1980; September 1980; December 17, 1981; December 1984.

Wickham, Martha B. Articles. *South Monmouth News*, October 18, 1951; November 1, 1951; November 8, 1951; December 6, 1951; December 13, 1951; January 17, 1952.

———. Unpublished articles of Captain Samuel Ludlow and the Brown family.

Worthington, Jean B. Interviews. August 26, 2010; December 5, 2010; assorted family scrapbooks and albums.

ABOUT THE AUTHOR

Lissa Wickham-McGrath is currently a member of Point Pleasant Historical Society, Sea Girt Lighthouse Society and Spring Lake Historical Society, as well as a PTO group. Lissa operated a women's shoe store in downtown Spring Lake for twenty years. She served as a regular feature writer for *Shore Holiday News* (no longer in print) and has worked on freelance writing projects for many local organizations.